From
Data to Dollars

**Turning Data Strategy
into Business Value**

Julia Bardmesser

Technics Publications
SEDONA, ARIZONA

TECHNICS PUBLICATIONS

115 Linda Vista, Sedona, AZ 86336 USA
https://www.TechnicsPub.com

Edited by Steve Hoberman
Cover design by Lorena Molinari
Author photo by Yan Li

First Printing 2025

Copyright © 2025 by Julia Bardmesser

ISBN, print ed.	9798898160128
ISBN, Kindle ed.	9798898160135
ISBN, PDF ed.	9798898160142

Library of Congress Control Number: 2025945399

In memory of my grandmother whose life continues to inspire me.

Acknowledgments

This book is the result of many years of hard-earned lessons, long days (and nights), thought-provoking conversations, and a deep belief that data can—and should—drive real business value.

There are so many people who supported and inspired this work, and I'm deeply grateful for all of them.

First, a heartfelt thank you to the incredible individuals who contributed their time, insights, and experience to the case studies featured in this book. Your real-world perspectives helped bring these stories to life and made the lessons far more grounded and impactful than any framework ever could. I want to especially thank:

Jane Conway
Yeon Lee
Eric Chacon
James Nichols
Fiona Humphrey

Thank you to Marina Severinovskaya and Olga Maydanchik for keeping me grounded in the messy, real-world complexities of building data capabilities. You consistently reminded me what it takes to make data work in practice, not just on paper.

I'm also grateful to Chris Adamson at TDWI, who believed early on in the "business value of data" concept. He gave me the opportunity to fully develop and test it in the classroom, and that support helped lay the foundation for this book.

To my colleagues, mentors, clients, and students—you have pushed my thinking, challenged my assumptions, and reminded me why this work matters.

Endorsements

Julia masterfully demonstrates how data serves as the ultimate litmus test of business strategy and execution. Her depth of knowledge is distilled into clear, actionable guidance that makes next steps feel like common sense.

Michelle Dunivan, Director of Analytics at Best Friends Animal Society

From Data to Dollars is a compelling and highly practical guide for any leader who wants to turn data into a true driver of business growth. Julia Bardmesser blends decades of real-world experience with clear, actionable frameworks, making even the most complex data strategies accessible and directly applicable. Through vivid case studies and relatable stories, she shows exactly how to align data initiatives with business goals so that value creation becomes inevitable. Whether you're an executive, a data leader, or a business strategist, this book will change how you think about—and act on—data.

Sherry Marcus, Head of AI at Tradeweb

Julia has written a book that is as valuable to the data practitioner as it is to the business leader. She clearly articulated concepts that link critical foundational data work to the business insights it enables. I'll be buying copies not just for my team, but for the business people we partner with.

Andrew Foster, CDO of M&T Bank

In the past decade, data and analytics resources for business leaders have grown rapidly — yet threading a cohesive data strategy that is co-authored and co-owned by business executives, data leaders, and technology delivery teams remains elusive for many enterprises. This book masterfully lays out the essential ingredients and step-by-step recipe for making that collaboration a reality. Through practical frameworks and relatable, cross-industry examples, the author empowers leaders to turn data into dollars by crafting value narratives that resonate across business and technology. A must-read for CTOs, CIOs, and CDAIOs seeking to build win-win partnerships with their business and segment heads, this is a quick yet powerful page-turner that combines clarity with actionable and measurable insights.

Kamayini Kaul, former Global CDO of Standard Chartered Bank

Contents

Introduction

The Chief Data Officer (CDO) world is full of dismal statistics:

- The average lifespan of a CDO in an organization is two years [1]
- The majority of all digital transformation initiatives fail.[2]

There are many reasons for these statistics, but in my experience, the major one is that managing data continues to be seen as a job for technologists, often accomplished out of sight and out of mind of the business. Yet, business leaders and data executives alike continue to ask the same question:

How do we extract value from data?

Many companies have taken steps they thought were necessary—hiring data leaders, building analytics teams, and implementing the latest data platforms—only to find themselves stuck and struggling to transform these investments into actionable insights that drive real business impact.

---

[1] https://hbr.org/2021/08/why-do-chief-data-officers-have-such-short-tenures.

[2] https://www.mckinsey.com/capabilities/transformation/our-insights/common-pitfalls-in-transformations-a-conversation-with-jon-garcia.

This book is about reframing data as a business strategy. The greatest barriers to achieving data-driven transformation are not technological, such as databases, Artificial Intelligence (AI) models, or reporting tools, but rather organizational: people and processes. The reality is that most enterprises do not suffer from scarcity of data. They grapple with misalignment of priorities, disconnects between data teams and business leaders, cultural resistance to change, and the absence of practical frameworks to seamlessly integrate data into strategic decision-making.

Consider that surveying CDOs consistently shows that the top barriers to data-driven success aren't technical limitations but organizational ones.[3] Misaligned incentives, unclear data ownership, and failure to prioritize data literacy across the company are what hold organizations back.

Simply put, data-driven transformation is a business transformation first and foremost, and like every business transformation, it requires executive buy-in, strategic direction, and a cultural shift.

I've spent over 25 years leading data and technology initiatives in large financial services companies, and I've witnessed this firsthand. I, too, have struggled to demonstrate the value of data initiatives, and I have also struggled to create a common understanding and alignment of incentives between business

---

[3] https://sloanreview.mit.edu/article/action-and-inaction-on-data-analytics-and-ai/.

teams and data and technology teams, continually trying to answer the "What's in it for me?" question.

This book represents crystallization of my best approaches and hard-won lessons on how to create this alignment, how to consistently nurture the understanding by the business of what they get out of data programs, not generally ("We get better data."), but specifically ("Here are my goals for this year and how I am going to be judged at the performance evaluation time, and here is how the data program enables me to achieve these goals.").

This book leverages a pragmatic, business case study-based approach to show you how to create that understanding and how to build a data capabilities strategy so closely aligned with business objectives that the question of "What is the ROI of data?" doesn't even come up—it's self-evident..

You'll learn:

- How to create a data strategy that aligns with real business objectives, not just technical aspirations.

- The role of leadership in driving a data-first culture and breaking down resistance to change.

- How to bridge the gap between technical teams and business stakeholders to ensure data is actually used in decision-making.

- Practical frameworks for improving data governance, quality, and usability so teams can trust and act on their data.

If your organization is struggling to make data a competitive advantage, you're not alone. Becoming truly data-driven goes beyond gathering more data—it requires a fundamental shift in how your company operates. This book will show you how to make that shift, step by step, in a way that drives meaningful, lasting business impact.

What about AI?

As I am writing this book, the world is in thrall of AI. The conversations range from "Is AI an existential threat to humanity?" to "Is it an existential threat to computer programmers?" to "Can AI solve all of our business problems, including fixing all of our data without us having to spend time or money on it?" The first two questions are outside of the purview of this book, while the answer to the third one is a qualified "no" – AI cannot solve all of the business or data problems, but it can, in fact, accelerate building data capabilities if used appropriately.

AI is a data capability.

It's a very powerful one, both the "old-style" predictive analytics and the newer generative AI. However, it's still a data capability.

Therefore, the approach to creating an AI strategy is the same as for the rest of the data capabilities: finding business value first, then defining a capability strategy that encompasses all necessary capabilities, including AI and GenAI, to deliver on that value. Throughout this book, whenever I mention reporting and analytics, I also include AI. Chapter 5 specifically highlights the additional possibilities that GenAI brings at different levels of data maturity.

PART ONE

Discovering Business Value

In Part 1, we examine the "why" of data strategy: how to uncover the business value of data for a company and what technical, organizational, and cultural capabilities a company needs to achieve its business goals.

CHAPTER ONE

Defining Data
and its Business Value

The central thesis of this book is that data strategy is business strategy. Like any business strategy, it must begin with a long-term vision, not isolated challenges. While addressing immediate issues (such as regulatory compliance or slow reporting cycles) may yield temporary fixes, a reactive approach fails to drive enduring, organization-wide transformation. An effective data strategy creates the greatest value when it aligns with the organization's overarching vision.

Vision

A company's strategic vision is a clear, aspirational statement that defines an organization's long-term direction and overarching purpose. It articulates *what* the organization aims to achieve in the future (its ultimate goal) and *why* it exists, serving as a north star to align decision-making, resource allocation, and priorities across all levels.

Why is knowing and aligning with the company's vision essential for driving data transformation and becoming data-driven?

A company's vision provides clarity and anchors decisions, priorities, and investments around a shared understanding of the destination.

Data initiatives often stall or pause in times of uncertainty and contraction. Clear articulation of value and alignment with the business vision enables these initiatives to remain prioritized and move forward even during challenging times and strained budgets.

Let me illustrate this with an example from my career. Following the 2008 financial crisis, every large financial institution worldwide launched a data program. These programs had clear objectives: to show regulators that the banks were safe, reduce the number and severity of regulatory actions and fines, and allow the banks to continue operating without being broken up. For the most part, they accomplished just that, and regulators were satisfied for a time. Yet, a few years later, regulatory scrutiny, along with fines and consent orders, returned to most of these banks that had declared victory over their data only a couple of years earlier. What happened? One common reason I have seen is that these programs were so closely associated with regulatory pressure that when this pressure eased a bit, people stopped paying so much attention to their data management discipline. It was considered "hygiene" or "nice to have," and businesses had other priorities. The data programs weren't aligned with the banks' vision and growth strategy; they were viewed as a cost of doing business in a specific geography.

Yet data strategy can and should be so much more.

In the chapters that follow, we will examine how an effectively executed data strategy helps advance and amplify an organization's strategic vision. It bears emphasizing that these elements are mutually reinforcing. In the absence of a clear vision, a data strategy lacks meaningful direction, while a vision ungrounded in data remains aspirational.

A company's vision serves as the anchor and guiding star of its business strategies.

Business Strategy

A company's business strategy is the translation of its strategic vision into action. If the vision defines *where* the company aspires to go and *why* it matters, then the business strategy defines *how* it will achieve this goal. The two are inseparable: strategy without vision is aimless; vision without strategy is just words on paper.

A business strategy determines which markets to enter or exit, which customer segments to serve, what value propositions to deliver, and what capabilities must be developed to support them. Ultimately, business strategy transforms ambition into execution.

Take, for example, a company whose strategic vision is to revolutionize personalized healthcare through technology. A business strategy built on that vision would need to answer critical questions. Should the company focus on AI-powered diagnostics, wearable health monitoring devices, or telemedicine platforms? Will it grow through acquisitions of biotech startups, internal research and development, or strategic partnerships with hospital systems? Will it lead with cost-effective solutions, cutting-edge innovation, or superior patient experience? Each of these decisions flow directly from the vision, shaped by market context, competitive positioning, and internal capabilities. The vision might be bold and inspiring, but to go beyond the rhetoric, it has to be grounded in specific business strategies.

Data Strategy

How does data strategy fit within business strategy overall?

Data is an internal capability just like sales, marketing, technology, and operational excellence. The state of data can either accelerate or stall a company's strategic vision. The aim of the business data strategy is to ensure it's the former and not the latter.

How do you align data strategy with the company's vision and its business strategy?

I call this process "Discovering Value."

What is the business value of data?

> *The business value of data is the contribution that data and data capabilities make to a company's bottom line.*

That immediately invites follow-up questions: What is data? And what is the difference between data and data capabilities?

Of course, there are many definitions of data out there, but I like this one from the Oxford language dictionary:

> *"Data are the things that are known or assumed as facts, making the basis of reasoning or calculation."*

Here are examples of different types of data a company may have:

Internal data:

- Customer information
- Product information
- Accounts and transactions
- Assets
- Distribution channel
- Profit and loss.

External data:

- Financial markets data
- Alternative data
- Vendor data
- Partner data

Metadata:

- Technical metadata (data attribute names, data access rules)
- Business metadata (business process names and descriptions, business terms, report descriptions)
- Data usage
- Data lineage.

Data Capabilities

But isn't data enough? Why are both data and data capabilities driving factors?

Let me tell you a story from my time as the head of data in a Fortune 500 company.

I just started my new job. Since it was a very senior position within the company, part of the onboarding process was to have "meets and greets" with the heads of all the business lines. During the interview process, I did my homework and was assured that there was broad executive support for a data program within the company. So off I went to meet the heads of businesses. The company had three major business lines. I had lovely and forward-looking conversations with the heads of two of them. However, things didn't go as smoothly when I met the CEO of the largest (and oldest) business line in the company. After I introduced myself, he said:

"Welcome! I am sure you'll like working here, it's a very nice place to work. I am, however, not quite sure what you plan to do here, at least for my business. You see, I have no problems with data. We have plenty of data, and I see it all the time. I do sometimes have problems with getting the reports done quickly, and sometimes I am not quite sure of the numbers. But data? No problem with it at all."

I was flabbergasted. This meeting took a few months to schedule, and by this time, I had already met several people from his business line. And, oh boy, did they have problems with data. This business had grown over many decades, often through mergers and acquisitions with little to no integration afterwards. I was so surprised that I couldn't answer him properly.

After another round of pleasantries, I left determined to work with his leaders to make progress. Which eventually happened, but that's a story for my next book.

So, how does this story show the importance of data capabilities? Because this leader unknowingly gave a perfect example of having data but not data capabilities, thus explaining their issues with reporting.

> *Data management capabilities make data that's already present in the company fully and reliably useful.*

The role of the Chief Data Officer isn't to create data but to make sure data can be used and trusted. CDOs build data capabilities and having data without data capabilities doesn't lead to value. You must have both.

So, what is a data capability?

This time around, I didn't see many good definitions when I googled the term, everything came back describing technology platforms. But ChatGPT gave a great definition:

> *Data capability refers to an organization's or system's ability to effectively and efficiently manage, analyze, interpret, and utilize data to support its objectives and decision-making processes. It encompasses the technological infrastructure, tools, processes, and skills required to collect, store, process, and extract insights from data.*

What's great about this definition? To define capabilities, it brings together people, processes, and technology. If you take nothing else from this book, remember this:

Merely possessing data is insufficient to unlock business value. Data must be both useful and usable—data capabilities are imperative for harnessing business value from data.

Data capabilities must extend beyond technology and encompass business and operational processes, as well as people.

Here are some examples of data capabilities:

Technical:

- Ability to collect data
- Ability to move data
- Ability to transform and combine data
- Ability to consume (that is, use) data.

Organizational:

- Understand the organization's data
- Understand when and how to use it
- Defined roles and responsibilities (for instance, data stewardship).

CHAPTER TWO

Business Value of a Data Framework

Let's consider the second part of our definition of the business value of data: the contribution that data and data capabilities make to the company's bottom line. We talked about data and data capabilities, now let's explore the bottom line. What factors influence a company's bottom line? In other words, how do companies grow?

For most for-profit companies, it boils down to a simple formula:

*Growth = more **customers** buy more of our **products** at a better **margin** and at an acceptable **risk**.*

GROWTH		
More Customers	**More Products**	**Better Margin**
New customer sales	Higher utilization of existing product	Operational efficiency
Customer retention	Buying additional products	Asset optimization
	Product innovation	
Acceptable Risk		

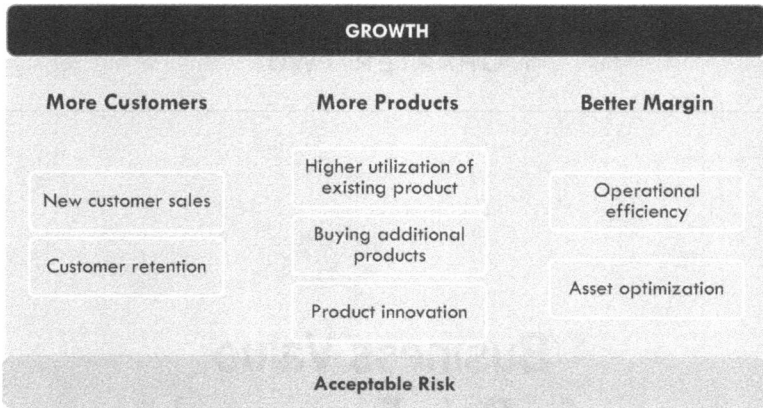

Figure 1: Growth = more customers buy more of our products at a better margin and at an acceptable risk.

Let's break this formula down one variable at a time.

More Customers

The first variable is **more customers**.

What does it mean to have more customers? Simply speaking, a company needs to attract new customers and retain existing ones. Both parts are important. Endless customer churn increases costs and inhibits growth. Similarly, not acquiring new customers, however well the company keeps old ones, inhibits growth.

Every company has customers. They may be called clients, partners, participants, or friends. If there are no customers, there is no business. This means that every business's vision touches on its relationship with its customers, and that vision translates into strategies and goals related to customer relationships. While the focus may change from year to year and from team to team, every growth-oriented business has at least one strategy—if not more— dedicated to expanding and retaining its customer base. Most business leaders today would wholeheartedly agree that data is crucial in their efforts to acquire and retain customers. However, most would struggle to identify which data capabilities are key to reaching their goals.

To illustrate, let me tell you another story from my experience.

After two years working at a company, I finally got a seat at the table in a joint business-technology digital strategy meeting, alongside my IT colleagues, the Head of Digital Technology and the Head of Business Applications. The business Head of Digital Strategy announced, "One of our goals this year is to increase the stickiness of our products by hyper-personalizing our client-facing website." I got super excited. We have already built a company-wide Client 360 platform that connected the information about all of our corporate customers and it was widely used across all business lines. We even had the funding to extend it to individual customers, but until now, there hadn't been a clear business case to justify it. And here it was, right in front of me. I almost jumped out of my chair:

"That's great! We can now extend our Master Data Management platform (aka client 360) to include individual customers."

The business executive looked at me blankly:

"What does it have to do with hyper-personalization? All we need is to add personalized digital widgets on our website and populate them with the data we already have, master data management isn't in scope."

That's what I got for letting my excitement get ahead of knowing my own stakeholders.

The point of this story is that my own understanding of how master data management enables hyper-personalization and supports customer retention wasn't enough; I also needed to create that understanding in everyone sitting around this table, from the business executive in charge to my technology peers. And not just the Head of Digital Strategy but also her teams, in their language, with a clear connection to their goals. That conversation was one of the inspirations for this book. I didn't explain it well at the time, so it took my team and me another couple of months for the executive to get fully on board. It was a challenge, so I want to make it easier for others who face similar conversations as I write this book. And yes, we did build Customer 360 for this program.

More Products

Moving on to the next variable, **more products**.

What does it mean to sell more of your product? Again, simply, it's either increasing the usage of your existing products or developing new products that create opportunities for cross-selling and reaching new customer segments.

Most business leaders recognize the importance of data for customer growth and retention. However, product leaders—unless the company specializes in selling data—often don't share the same understanding. This is particularly true when a company's products are services, for example:

- Investment advice
- Deposits, mortgages, and loans
- Management consulting
- IT services
- Package delivery.

Many companies lack a centralized, well-maintained digital repository of their products. As a result, their websites feature poorly organized lists of products and services that aren't linked to what salespeople see in their Customer Relationship Management (CRM) system. Which in turn aren't connected to the pricing system, and none of these are connected to the onboarding systems. This lack of integration not only creates significant manual effort for operational and sales teams, but it also hinders the company's ability to understand product profitability and effectively cross-sell.

This creates a challenging paradox: while product master data is one of the most impactful and quickest-to-market data management capabilities to build, it is often the hardest to explain to the business and gain full participation from them.

A data strategy focused on these two pillars—customer and product—is often referred to as Data Offense. One of the interesting subsets of the Data Offense strategy is data monetization.

> *Data monetization uses data from existing, mature business lines to create new products or business lines that attract diverse customers while improving margins.*

This is an especially important strategy for legacy companies in industries with shrinking margins. Later in this book, I will explore a case study that examines this challenge and demonstrates how data management capabilities support this type of strategy.

The next growth variable, **margin**, is perhaps the most intuitively connected to data, but it's not as straightforward as it seems.

First, are better margins necessary for growth? Well, that depends on how you define growth. If growth is defined by an expanding customer base, increasing revenue, or geographical reach, then margin doesn't really come into play. In the past ten years, with the rise of so-called digital giants, we have seen explosive growth and high valuations of the companies that poured all of their revenues into customer or geography growth, paying little attention to margins. Uber is a well-known example of this phenomenon. Many of us fondly remember the days when it was possible to get around LA for very little money without any need to own a car.

Of course, this eventually stopped. After Uber went public, it had to show not just revenue growth but also generate profits.

Setting these exceptions aside, the margin is very important to the true growth of the company. True, sustainable growth only occurs when revenue exceeds expenses. Otherwise, companies eventually fold or get bought.

What are the levers that drive operational efficiency to improve margins, and how can they be influenced or enhanced by establishing data management capabilities?

There are countless ways in which effective data management can improve operational efficiency. Let me discuss two examples that I have seen in my career.

First and foremost, it's straight-through processing: the automation of business processes that allows data to flow seamlessly and efficiently from one step to the next without requiring manual intervention. This reduces manual adjustments and corrections across operational processes from start to finish. The most common reasons for manual adjustments are poor data quality in operational systems, incomplete data, or data mismatches caused by differing expectations between the process generating the data, and the consuming process. For example, in an ecommerce company, the inventory management system may show a product as "in stock" based on warehouse quantities, but the order fulfillment system expects this status to also account for items already allocated to pending orders that haven't yet shipped. When a customer places an order for what appears to be available inventory, the system discovers the item is actually unavailable, requiring manual intervention to cancel the order, update inventory records, and handle customer communications.

Call center costs are a major challenge for many companies. Many businesses operate large-scale call centers, and even when located in lower-cost regions, these operations represent a substantial expense. Leveraging data capabilities can dramatically boost efficiency and profit margins.

A key metric for call center efficiency is the average amount of time a representative spends on the phone with a customer. This metric is often used to evaluate the performance of call centers and their managers.

A major time sink for a call center representative is the need to find customer information across multiple systems. The more systems they have to consult, the more screens and documents they need to answer a customer's question, the worse their time metric becomes. Data management in general, and GenAI in particular, are powerful capabilities that can have a direct impact on improving this metric.

Acceptable Risk

The last dimension of the growth formula is **acceptable risk.**

Every company must manage its risks. Please note, I say manage, not eliminate. Almost by definition, running a business means taking risks. Operational risks, financial risks, regulatory risks, credit risks, etc. Each of these risk types must be managed—if left unattended, they can destroy the company (remember Enron?), but they must also be controlled just enough to avoid hindering growth and risk-taking. For instance, a pharmaceutical company faces significant regulatory risk if it cannot trace exactly where every batch of its drugs is in the supply chain and verify that all production steps meet strict compliance standards. To manage that risk, the company needs strong data management capabilities in place to respond quickly to a regulator's request, prove compliance, and even act preemptively when an issue arises, avoiding fines, recalls, or reputational damage, while still moving new products to market quickly.

Data management programs often start with risk management mandates, especially in highly regulated industries such as banking and pharmaceuticals.

While a data strategy focused on the customer and product is called Data Offense, a data strategy for risk management is called Data Defense. This strategy focuses on streamlining the data necessary to understand and manage risks within the company.

Now that we've defined the value framework, let's deep dive into the case studies that exemplify how data capabilities enable companies to create value in each of these dimensions.

CHAPTER THREE

Business Case Studies

Case Study 1: Risk Weighted Assets (RWA)

Risk-Weighted Assets (RWA) determine the amount of capital a bank must set aside to cover potential losses. Regulators enforce these rules to ensure banks can absorb financial shocks and protect depositors. But for banks, these requirements present a strategic challenge: holding too much capital limits profitability, while holding too little risks regulatory penalties and financial instability.

Risk-Weighted Assets represent the total assets of a bank, adjusted for risk. Instead of treating all assets equally, regulators assign different risk weights based on asset type, borrower creditworthiness, and other financial risk factors. The higher the risk, the more capital a bank must set aside.

Why is it important for a bank to understand its RWA?

First: it's a regulatory requirement.

Banks operate in a heavily regulated environment, where they must comply with capital adequacy standards set by global frameworks, such as Basel III. These rules are designed to prevent financial crises by ensuring banks have enough capital to cover unexpected losses. If a bank fails to meet these requirements, it could face penalties, restrictions on business activities, or, in extreme cases, insolvency.

Second, it's a core part of maintaining financial resilience. Accurate risk assessment allows banks to understand the true exposure across their portfolios, ensuring they can absorb losses without threatening day-to-day operations. Inaccurate calculations can mask vulnerabilities, leading to liquidity crunches or sudden write-downs that erode stakeholder confidence.

And third, it's key to making strategic growth decisions. Well-calibrated capital planning lets banks direct resources toward the most promising opportunities while maintaining an appropriate safety buffer. This balance supports both regulatory compliance and the ability to pursue lending, investments, or new business lines that fuel long-term growth.

The goal is to strike the right balance, ensuring enough capital is set aside for safety while maximizing the amount available for growth.

It's beyond the scope of this book to present all the data and analytics required to complete the RWA calculation for all asset types in a bank. This business study will use the example of a corporate loan to show that to solve the RWA challenge, a well-thought-out and executed data strategy is a must.

Let's examine data and data capabilities needed by a bank to determine the minimum capital required for a $20 million loan to a corporate entity.

What information is needed to calculate the RWA for a loan?

First, we need information about the loan itself, such as:

- Original loan balance
- Remaining balance of the loan
- Maturity date
- Collateral information
- Currency information.

Why is this information important in evaluating the risk of the loan?

Let's look at the maturity date as an example.

The maturity of a loan—the length of time until it is fully repaid—affects the RWA calculation because longer-term loans typically carry higher risk. Regulators and banks consider maturity in RWA calculations due to its impact on default probability, interest rate risk, credit risk, and capital requirements. Here's why:

Longer Maturity Means Higher Default Risk

The longer a loan remains outstanding, the greater the uncertainty about whether the borrower will be able to repay it. Over time, a company's financial health can change due to economic downturns, industry shifts, or internal mismanagement.

For example:

- A one-year loan has a lower chance of running into borrower financial distress than a ten-year loan, simply because less can go wrong in the shorter period.

- A long-term loan to a company in a volatile industry (for instance, oil and gas) faces higher risk because market conditions can fluctuate significantly over time.

Due to this increased uncertainty, longer-term loans are assigned higher risk weights, which require banks to hold more capital.

Exposure to Interest Rate Risk

Interest rate fluctuations can impact a borrower's ability to repay long-term debt. For example, a company that takes out a floating rate loan might struggle to repay it if rates increase, leading to a higher default risk.

From a bank's perspective:

- A longer loan locks in risk for an extended period, making it harder to adjust pricing or risk exposure.

- Regulatory frameworks, such as Basel III, apply maturity adjustments to capture this risk, requiring more capital for loans with extended maturities.

Lower Flexibility for Banks

Short-term loans give banks the flexibility to reprice risk more frequently, adjusting for changes in a borrower's creditworthiness or market conditions. Longer-maturity loans lock in risk exposure, meaning banks must hold capital for a prolonged period without the ability to adjust terms easily.

This is particularly important in volatile economic environments; if a downturn occurs, a long-term loan can become a significant liability on a bank's balance sheet.

How do regulatory frameworks treat maturity dates?

Basel III and other regulatory frameworks apply a maturity adjustment when calculating RWA, particularly for loans with maturities greater than one year. The general rule is:

- **Short-term loans (<1 year)**: Lower risk weight because there is less exposure to uncertainty.

- **Medium-term loans (1-5 years)**: Moderate risk weight, depending on the borrower's credit profile.

- **Long-term loans (>5 years)**: Higher risk weight due to increased exposure to credit and market risks.

In some cases, Basel III applies a maturity factor in the RWA formula, where a longer loan amplifies the capital requirement. Remember these risk weights, we will talk about them again when discussing the importance of data quality later in this chapter. However, just knowing the details about the loan isn't enough to calculate an accurate RWA.

Another very important category of information is what we know about the counterparty (often called the obligor by risk departments). Here are some examples of data that's needed about the counterparty:

- Internal credit rating
- Client tenure
- Industry code
- Country of operations
- External credit rating.

Why is counterparty information important to determine RWA?

Let's use the country of operations to illustrate the importance of counterparty information, When a bank assesses the Risk-Weighted Assets (RWA) for a loan, one key factor is where the borrower (obligor) operates. The country of operations influences the risk level associated with the loan, which directly impacts how much capital the bank must hold against it. Here's why:

Economic and Political Stability

The economic health and political environment of a country significantly impact a company's ability to repay its debt. Loans to borrowers in stable, developed economies are generally considered lower risk because of strong legal frameworks, well-established financial systems, and stable government policies. In contrast, lending to a company operating in a country with high inflation, frequent political unrest, or weak regulatory oversight carries more risk. If an economy crashes or a government enforces capital controls, borrowers may struggle to repay their debts, increasing the likelihood of default. This higher risk means the loan is assigned a higher risk weight, requiring the bank to hold more capital.

Sovereign Risk and Credit Ratings

Every country has a sovereign credit rating, which indicates its ability to meet financial obligations. Countries with high credit ratings (for instance, AAA from S&P or Aaa from Moody's) signal strong economic fundamentals and low default risk. Loans made to obligors in these countries typically receive lower risk weights.

On the other hand, if a country has a low credit rating or is at risk of default, the businesses operating there may face economic pressures that make repayment uncertain. In such cases, banks must assign a higher risk weight to reflect this increased exposure to sovereign risk.

Currency and Foreign Exchange Risk

If a borrower operates in a country with an unstable currency or fluctuating exchange rates, their ability to repay a loan could be compromised. For example:

- If a company earns revenue in a weak local currency but has debt obligations in U.S. dollars, a sudden depreciation of the local currency can make it much harder for them to service their debt.

- Some governments impose capital controls, restricting how much money businesses can transfer out of the country, which can impact loan repayments.

Banks must consider these risks when calculating RWA and may assign higher risk weights to loans in countries with volatile currency markets.

Legal and Regulatory Frameworks

Different countries have different laws governing bankruptcy, debt recovery, and creditor protections. In countries with robust legal systems, banks have a better chance of recovering funds if a borrower defaults, resulting in a lower risk weight. However, in countries where debt enforcement is weak or government intervention is unpredictable, banks may find it difficult to recover losses. In such cases, loans to obligors in these regions are considered riskier, requiring higher capital reserves to cover potential losses.

Industry-Specific Risks Tied to Geography

Some industries are more exposed to country-specific risks. For example:

- A mining company operating in a politically unstable country faces risks of government expropriation or sudden policy changes.

- A manufacturer in a country subject to international sanctions may face restricted access to global markets, affecting their ability to generate revenue and repay loans.

Banks must factor in these risks when assigning RWA to loans, adjusting capital requirements accordingly.

In addition to loan and counterparty information, payment history, and details about other products and services that obligors have with the bank are also taken into account to accurately calculate RWA.

Why do the obligor's other products and services impact RWA? Here are some of the reasons:

Counterparty Risk Across Different Products

Many corporate clients utilize additional financial services, including derivatives, trade finance, and treasury management.

If the obligor has high-risk exposures in any of these categories, the RWA for a corporate loan could be adjusted upward to reflect the overall credit risk.

Collateral and offsetting Positions

Some products that the obligor holds with the bank might reduce RWA if they provide risk mitigation:

- Deposits and Cash Collateral: If the obligor maintains large deposits with the bank, these can be used as collateral to offset loan exposure, lowering RWA.

- Offsetting Derivatives Positions: If the obligor has opposing derivative contracts that reduce net exposure, this may decrease counterparty credit risk.

Conversely, if the obligor has unsecured exposure across multiple financial products, the RWA may increase due to the greater risk of loss.

Past Payment Behavior and Credit Deterioration

- If the obligor has a history of late payments or financial distress in other accounts, the bank may apply a higher risk weight to reflect the increased likelihood of default.

- If the obligor has consistently met its obligations across multiple products, the bank might be more comfortable with a lower risk weight, depending on internal credit assessment models.

In summary, to accurately calculate the RWA of a corporate loan, the bank must have a wide variety of data, including information about loans both at origination and in their current state, information about the borrower that includes indicative information such as their country of operations or external credit rating and also their up-to-date payment history and other products and services they may have with the banks.

Figure 2 shows how the RWA calculation information map can be represented graphically.

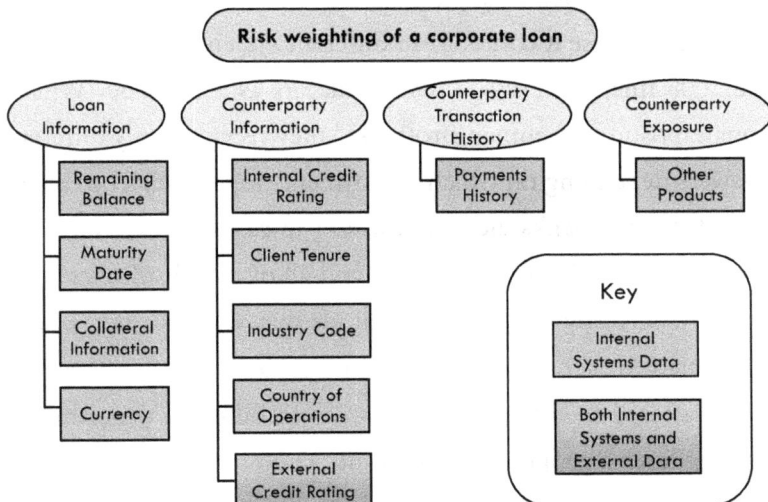

Figure 2: In this capital management example, the goal is to accurately perform a risk-weighted calculation for a $20 million loan to a corporate entity.

Now that we understand what data is needed to calculate RWA, what are the data capabilities necessary and why?

Let's start by finding the right place to get all the data we need for RWA.

In most banks, it resides in many systems that are owned and supported by different business and technology teams. For example, loan origination information, such as the original balance and maturity date, usually resides in loan onboarding systems, while collateral information is often found in a separate system. The current balance is most often calculated in various transaction processing systems. Knowing which of these systems has the most accurate and up-to-date information is no small task, and it's common for different teams across risk and finance to receive information that ought to be the same but is, in fact, different because it comes from different systems. In fact, during the 2008 financial crisis, when regulators asked banks, "What's your exposure to Lehman Brothers?" they received very different answers depending on which department responded. The reason wasn't that the banks didn't know how to calculate exposure, the reason was that Lehman Brothers and all of its subsidiaries were a) represented by multiple internal ids that were not necessarily connected to each other, b) information about Lehman Brothers was scattered in different systems across different departments and different geographies with no companywide knowledge which of these systems had the correct and up to date information.

So, just knowing what data is needed isn't enough; as the very first step, we need to know what the right sources are to get this data from. **Data governance** enables the organization to identify and codify which business processes and underlying systems generate data that other businesses and functions can appropriately utilize, and to maintain this list as the business and technology landscape evolves.

This is one of the reasons why data governance programs are featured prominently in many banks' responses to regulatory concerns.

Data governance, though, isn't the only data capability needed to get to the accurate RWA result.

Just knowing where the correct data resides isn't enough; we need to be able to use this data collectively to perform the RWA calculations. This means that we need to connect the data from the loan origination system to the data from the loan transaction system, as well as the data about the counterparty for this specific loan. All of this data is produced by different business processes that are mostly independent of each other. This means that there is no naturally occurring mechanism that would create common keys connecting all this data.

What is a common key?

A common key is a field that serves as a link between multiple records, connecting related pieces of data. It helps identify which records belong together. In our case study, the customer ID serves as a common key that ties the loan record in the originating system to the customer record in the customer database and to the transaction system that processes the monthly loan payment. **Master Data Management (MDM)** is a data capability that creates, maintains, and distributes common keys for the most important entities within the company. Keep in mind that any type of business outcome that needs to bring together data created by more than one business process requires this ability to link related entities to produce accurate results.

For the companies that have not established MDM as a data capability, this work is usually done manually, time- and labor-intensively, with often inconsistent outcomes. The lack of scalable common keys (that is, MDM) is one of the major reasons for the breaks in the straight through processing, and lack of consistency in different reports and analytics, and thus the lack of trust in using data for decision making.

The third major data capability needed to solve our RWA challenge is **Data Quality Management**. Data Quality Management is the ability to understand which level of data quality is appropriate for different business purposes within the enterprise and create processes to measure and remediate the data that doesn't meet the required level of quality.

Data quality is especially important in the case of RWA because of regulatory rules requiring the use of the most conservative defaults if the key piece of information is missing. For example, if the country of operations is not known, the RWA calculation must assign weights as if it's the worst-case scenario country, thus increasing the amount of capital that has to be put aside and correspondingly reducing the amount of active capital—that is, reducing the bank's ability to make money. This requirement establishes a direct connection between the quality of clients and loan data, and the bank's profitability.

In summary, in addition to data, to achieve accurate and trusted RWA calculations, banks require robust data capabilities to ensure accuracy, consistency, and usability. **Data governance** provides the foundation by defining and maintaining authoritative data sources across the organization. **Master Data Management (MDM)** facilitates the necessary linkages between disparate datasets, ensuring that records can be accurately connected across systems. Finally, **Data Quality Management** ensures that the data used for calculations meets the required standards, preventing costly regulatory penalties and helping banks avoid setting aside excessive capital.

Without these capabilities, banks face significant challenges: they may use incorrect or outdated data sources, struggle to connect related information across systems, or default to conservative regulatory requirements that tie up capital unnecessarily. While implementing these capabilities requires significant investment and organizational change, the alternative—manual processes, inconsistent reporting, and inefficient capital allocation—is far more costly in the long run. As the 2008 financial crisis demonstrated with Lehman Brothers, the absence of robust data capabilities goes beyond an operational inconvenience. It becomes a fundamental risk to both individual institutions and the broader financial system.

Case Study 2: Data Offense Sales Acceleration

Following the 2008 crisis, regulators made it clear that robust data management was essential for regulatory reporting and compliance. Many banks made significant investments in response, and, not unreasonably, a few years down the road, they started considering how to leverage that investment not just for regulatory compliance but also for the bank's growth.

Moreover, as data management practices gained prominence— and with the rise and widespread adoption of big data technologies, along with the resulting surge in 3Vs (data volume, velocity, and variety), companies across various industries began exploring how to leverage data to gain a competitive edge and drive growth.

In this case study, we'll discuss one of the most commonly used methods for growing the company: acquiring more customers.

In the journey from potential interest to a completed sale, businesses have long relied on a model known as the marketing and sales funnel. The term "funnel" is apt, symbolizing the reality that while many may show initial interest, only a fraction of them will ultimately make a purchase.

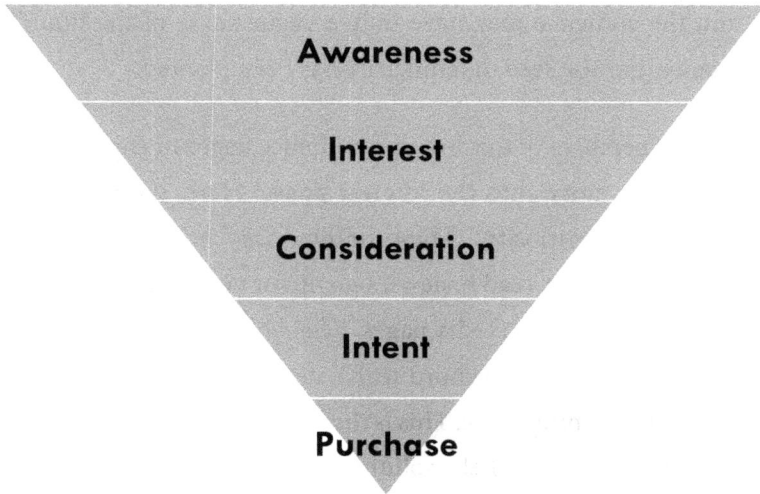

Figure 3: The traditional marketing and sales funnel.

This model helps businesses understand how prospects progress through different stages of engagement and where they may encounter obstacles that prevent further progression.

The funnel is divided into a series of stages, each representing a distinct phase in the customer decision-making process. While specific terminology may vary, the core concepts remain largely consistent across industries.

At the top of the funnel lies the awareness stage. This is where the journey begins. Potential customers first encounter the brand through various channels, including digital advertising, social media posts, blog articles, podcasts, influencer mentions, and even word of mouth. The primary objective here is visibility. A business must ensure that its product, service, or value proposition becomes known to those who may eventually need it. At this point, the audience may have only a vague sense of the brand's existence, but the seed of familiarity has been planted.

As some members of this broader audience begin to engage more deeply, they move into the interest phase. Here, the brand has piqued their curiosity. These individuals may explore the company's website, read reviews, sign up for newsletters, or follow the company's social media pages. Their behavior indicates that the offering has struck a chord with a need or desire, and they are receptive to learning more. This is the stage where informative and engaging content can help solidify the brand's relevance to the customer's life or business challenges.

The next stage—consideration—is where prospects become more deliberate in their actions. They now actively assess the offering. They may compare features, analyze pricing, request demos, or seek testimonials. In this middle portion of the funnel, the customer is asking a critical question: "Is this the right choice for me?" Companies must be prepared to support this evaluation process by providing credible information, demonstrating value, and addressing any potential objections. This is often the stage where trust is either built or lost.

As evaluation gives way to intent, the customer's behavior becomes more serious. They might reach out for a quote, begin negotiations, or seek approval from internal stakeholders if they're part of an organization. These signals indicate that the customer is preparing to buy, but this phase can also be a point where momentum stalls. Internal politics, budget constraints, or competing priorities can derail even the most promising opportunities. This is the stage where sales teams must be both persuasive and supportive, helping the customer move smoothly toward a commitment.

At the bottom of the funnel lies the moment of conversion: the purchase. After navigating all previous stages, the customer finally completes the transaction. While this marks the culmination of the traditional funnel journey, it should not be seen as the end of the relationship. In fact, what happens after the purchase, including onboarding, customer support, and ongoing engagement, can significantly influence retention, satisfaction, and long-term brand loyalty.

To explore the complexities of marketing and sales funnel dynamics in a real-world setting, consider the case of BestPlatform Inc. (a fictitious name used to protect confidentiality), an enterprise technology firm specializing in selling enterprise software solutions to other businesses. As a B2B (business-to-business) provider, BestPlatform's success depends not only on the quality of its products but also on its ability to effectively guide potential customers through all the stages of their buyer journey.

Each stage of this journey brings its own unique set of challenges, and in the context of enterprise software, these obstacles are often magnified. Deals can be complex, sales cycles are long, and decision-making involves multiple stakeholders. For companies like BestPlatform, the early stages of the funnel, when potential customers are just beginning to engage, can be particularly difficult to navigate.

Awareness: The Challenge of Being Seen and Heard

At the top of the funnel lies the awareness stage, where the primary goal is visibility. Amid the noise of the digital age, capturing audience attention poses a greater challenge than in the past.

BestPlatform faced three major hurdles at this stage:

- **Audience fragmentation:** The modern media landscape is highly fragmented, with buyers consuming content across a wide range of platforms, including social media, professional networks, podcasts, email newsletters, and niche industry websites, among others. For marketing teams at BestPlatform, this dispersion made it difficult to pinpoint where their target audience spends time. Without a clear understanding of where and how to engage prospective buyers (that is, optimizing the **channel**), even the most compelling messaging was often going unheard.

- **Content saturation:** Even when the right channels were identified, BestPlatform had to contend with the sheer volume of content already competing for attention. Their potential customers were inundated with marketing messages from every direction. Standing out required an acute understanding of what would resonate—that is, optimizing the **message**. Generic messaging would simply not cut through the noise.

- **Attribution uncertainty:** Perhaps the most insidious challenge was determining what was actually working. Marketing leaders often struggled to connect specific awareness efforts—whether a LinkedIn ad, a webinar, or a thought leadership article—to meaningful downstream outcomes. Without clear attribution, it was difficult to optimize spending or justify the value of top-of-funnel activities. Misallocated budgets led to an inefficient strategy, even if individual tactics were executed well.

Interest and Consideration: The Hurdle of Relevance

As prospects moved further into the funnel, their interactions became more focused as they began researching solutions, evaluating options, and forming early preferences.

The Relevance Gap

Creating content that aligned with the specific needs and questions of prospects at this point in their journey required a deep understanding of the audience's mindset. Unfortunately, many organizations fall short here. Content is often too broad, too technical, or too generic, missing the opportunity to build trust and demonstrate value. For BestPlatform, narrowing this "relevance gap" was a top priority, demanding better buyer persona information, more targeted messaging, and tighter alignment between marketing and sales.

Inefficient Lead Qualification

Even when interest was expressed through downloads, demo requests, or email engagement, not all leads are created equal. BestPlatform had struggled at times to accurately identify which prospects were truly sales-ready and which were unlikely to convert. Without effective lead scoring and qualification processes, sales teams found themselves chasing poor-fit prospects while high-potential opportunities slipped through the cracks. The result was wasted effort, lower conversion rates, and unnecessary strain on the organization's sales team.

As part of its business growth strategy to increase its customer base, BestPlatform set a goal for its distribution team: to increase the product sales to new customers by 50% without increasing the number of salespeople. The distribution team determined that to achieve this goal, they would utilize data and analytics to identify the right customers for their products, engage with them at the right time with the right message over the most effective channel.

Let's start with how they determined who the right customer was.

The first question they asked was: "How do we know they are ready for our type of product?"

There were several ways to obtain this information, starting with customer lists of similar products (for instance, having a list of Oracle customers would give a starting point to the makers of a new cloud-based data warehousing platform). Then, to further refine this list, public information about the target prospects' strategy could be used. For example, if the company mentioned during quarterly analyst calls that it was undergoing cloud or digital transformation, it was a good bet that they were evaluating their data footprint and were open to new vendors. Additionally, salespeople's industry knowledge and familiarity with key players could further refine the prospect list.

Was this information enough to focus salespeople's efforts? Not quite. The next question the team asked was, "Who is the decision maker?"

Why was that important? Let me share another story from my time as a data leader at a Fortune 500 company. I was often invited to dinners by data product vendors. I didn't always go, but there was one invitation that caught my eye: it was in a very well-known and highly rated restaurant close to my home. The invitation wasn't overly specific; it had no vendor name, just come to a great dinner and discuss information management with your peers from other institutions.

So, I went, and it was, in fact, a great dinner. Great food, a separate room with good acoustics, allowing everyone around the table to hear each other, and thoughtful, non-salesy moderation from the vendor. It was enjoyable and educational. But from a vendor's perspective, my presence there was a complete waste of money. They were selling an information security platform, not an information management platform. An information security vendor's target market is the CISO (Chief Information Security Officer), not the CDO (Chief Data Officer). I did send the information about them to my company's CISO, but it didn't work out. The moral of the story: If the goal is to focus sales and marketing efforts to accelerate the sales process, the decision maker's role and name are very important.

How would BestPlatform determine the decision maker? Similar to the readiness question, salesperson knowledge, public filings, and social media posts all offer insight into this information.

Is that enough? Almost, but not quite yet. One more important data point: has the customer shown any interest in our products? This information would come from tracking potential prospects' engagement on the website, webinar signups, white paper downloads, and last but not least, interest at conferences.

To recap, BestPlatform aimed to boost new customer sales by 50% without adding sales staff. They used data to identify the right clients by asking:

- **Are they ready?** Look for signs like the use of similar products or digital transformation goals.

- **Who decides?** Target the actual decision maker, not just any exec.

- **Are they interested?** Track engagement, such as site visits or event signups.

This approach helped focus sales efforts on where they'd have the most impact. Let's summarize with a "Who is the right customer?" information map. See Figure 4.

This set of information served as a strong foundation for BestPlatform's sales acceleration strategy. But in order to use it effectively and deliver a daily list of likely prospects to each salesperson, they had to fulfil the following requirements:

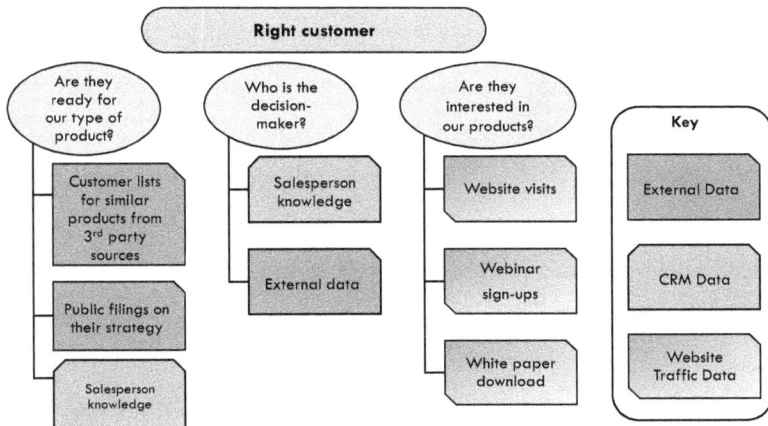

Figure 4: Tech company: How do we know who is the right client?

First, they had to apply data governance to identify reliable sources of external information. But how exactly does data governance help here? Can't the business just do the research, find the sources, and be done with it? That's often the typical approach to bringing external information into a company. However, that approach assumes the quality of those sources won't change or that no better sources will emerge.

Data governance addresses this by assigning business data owners who are accountable for monitoring the quality of these sources and staying informed about any new and improved alternatives. For data offense use cases, data governance stops being about compliance or hygiene; it, instead, starts playing its proper role as an enabler of value, of ensuring the system continuously delivers the best possible results.

In addition to external sources of information, salespeople's knowledge is very important. CRM (Customer Relationship Management) platforms are commonly deployed to extract this information from the minds of salespeople and operationalize it for insight and tracking. However, salespeople generally view updating the CRM as a hassle—something that takes time away from engaging with prospects. Establishing data quality rules for CRM data and linking data quality scores to the success of the sales acceleration strategy and ultimately to compensation can go a long way in fostering a culture where salespeople consistently update the CRM accurately and promptly.

> *Defining the key CRM data attributes required for the sales acceleration strategy, establishing appropriate data quality rules, determining the consequences of not meeting quality thresholds, and then measuring performance to produce relevant and actionable insights—these are all essential components of a robust data quality management capability.*

Once we have identified the best sources of external information and created an environment where CRM updates are timely and current, what else is needed to generate an accurate and actionable list of likely prospects?

Similar to the RWA case study, we need to be able to meaningfully combine external data, CRM data, and website traffic data to make sure we correctly identify prospects. This is not a simple matter. External sources, internal CRM, and website traffic identifiers all have different naming conventions. In other words, creating a master data management discipline around prospects is just as important for this use case as it is for the RWA use case. The complexity, of course, is that even if we were to apply this business challenge to a bank (and it is highly transferable) that has already invested in a client master data management system to address the RWA challenge, this bank would face new hurdles. While the underlying capability remains the same and its existence can save significant time and resources, the actual data to be mastered differs. It comes primarily from external sources, has different attributes, and requires different rules for disambiguating entities.

> *This highlights the central point that to drive meaningful impact with data, both high-quality data and strong data capabilities are essential.*

Let's explore this further through an example of a bank that has already built robust data governance, data quality, and master data management capabilities for RWA and is now extending its data strategy to accelerate sales in its corporate banking line of business.

Figure 5 shows how the "right client" information map would look for corporate banking services.

While there are some similarities between the data required for RWA and identifying the right client, this information comes from different sources. RWA relies primarily on internal systems, whereas identifying prospects requires external sources that provide information about potential clients.

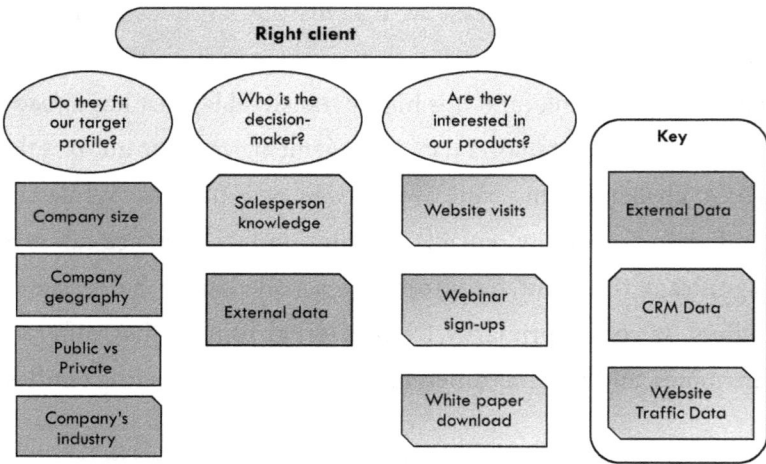

Figure 5: Corporate banking: How do we know who is the right client?

Let's compare and contrast each of the capabilities for these two business cases.

Data Governance:

Sample actions	RWA	Sales acceleration	Changes required?
Policy and standards	Same	Same	No
Stewardship roles and responsibilities	Same	Same	No
Source data stewards	Business and ops that are responsible for the internal data	Business and ops that are responsible for CRM and external sources	Yes
Consumption data stewards	Corporate Risk	Marketing and sales	Yes

As we can see, while enterprise-wide data governance artifacts—such as policies, standards, and overall stewardship roles and responsibilities—are applicable to both use cases, a new set of individuals would need to be selected for the stewardship roles to extend the data governance capability to this new business case.

The changes extend further when we consider the Master Data Management capability:

Sample actions	RWA	Sales acceleration	Changes required?
Platform selection	Same	Same	No
Source data ingestion	Internal systems	External feeds +CRM	Yes
Disambiguation (match&merge) rules	Similar: rules would likely use the name and address of a company, but physical attributes would differ	Similar	Yes, but not significant
Mastered data integration	Risk RWA engine	Analytics and CRM systems	Yes

Again, we can see that significant portions of the Master Data capabilities built for RWA can be leveraged for the sales acceleration use case. However, it's not a straightforward effort: both the data sources to be mastered and the consuming systems that require this master data are very different. This once again emphasizes the critical lesson about data versus data capability: both are necessary to create value from data. Having a data capability that doesn't handle the type or source of data required for a new use case isn't helpful. Likewise, just having data coming from different sources without a way to connect it automatically and at scale, greatly hinders the value a company can extract from that data.

Let's go back to our BestPlatform tech company and see what happened after they built a data and analytics engine to identify the prospects that are most likely to become customers. That was already a huge step in accelerating their sales journey. However, that wasn't enough. Their next step was to extend the system to identify the right channel for engaging the prospect. After all, reaching out to the likeliest prospect over a phone that is never answered doesn't get you a sale.

This addition went smoothly since many organizational and technical capabilities had already been established in this area.

How could BestPlatform identify the right channel to reach the likely prospect?

First, they could ask! And keep that information in the preference tracking system that would be connected to their authoritative source of prospect and customer data. (A side note on data architecture: a "prospect" and a "customer" are usually distinguished by a status field and the specific product or service they've purchased. For this reason, it's often best to manage both in the same system.)

The second source of channel preference information was the salesperson's knowledge. Since CRM stewardship, DQ rules, and governance have been established in Phase I ("the right customer"), it's easy to extend it to this attribute as well. The stewards were in place, data quality measurement was in place, and most importantly, the tie-in between data quality and salespersons' KPIs was in place as well.

But there was more information available beyond "digital" or "in-person" channel selection. By leveraging modern digital engagement tracking technologies and effectively using website activity tags, BestPlatform could find out whether emails are effective, whether webinars get more attention, or whitepapers generate the most interest for this specific prospect. Similarly, by leveraging the discipline that's been built around CRM updates, information on responsiveness to phone calls or in-person meetings and events could also be added to the mix. Figure 6 shows the "What is the right channel?" information map.

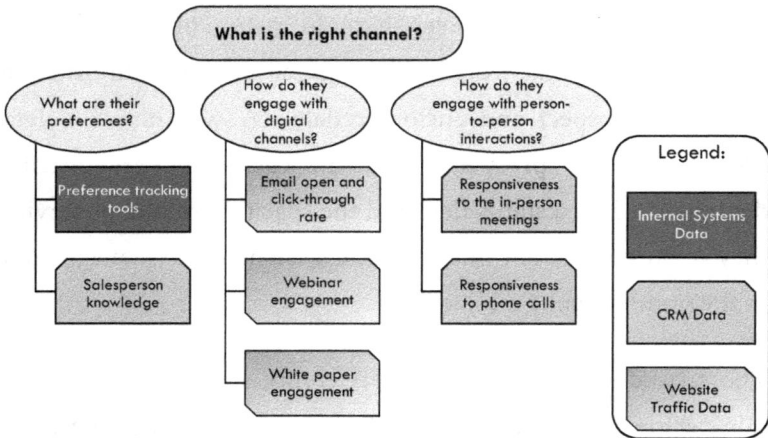

Figure 6: Tech company: The output "find the right channel" process is the channel indicator for each of the clients.

The addition of this information to the sales acceleration platform was not a big deal from either an organizational or technological capabilities perspective, given CRM data governance had been put in place to ensure the completeness and correctness of the data entered by salespeople. Both the CRM system and website traffic data were already connected to the intelligence platform, and there were no changes required to master the prospect data. There were two main changes here: one is to build the preference tracking system and connect it to the intelligence platform, and the second is to create an analytical model to provide a correct prediction of the most likely channel to elicit a positive response from a prospect.

This sales acceleration case study illustrates a fundamental principle that creating business value with data requires both the right data and mature data capabilities working in concert. Neither is sufficient alone.

The journey from identifying the "right customer" to determining the "right channel," "right time," and "right message" demonstrated how foundational data disciplines create compounding returns when thoughtfully deployed. What started as a targeted effort to identify promising prospects evolved into a comprehensive intelligence platform driving the entire sales funnel.

Here are the key takeaways from this case study:

- Data governance isn't just for defense—when properly implemented, it becomes the critical enabler for offensive data strategies by ensuring data quality, stewardship, and continuous improvement in both internal and external data sources.

- Master data management capabilities built for a single business case (such as regulatory compliance) provide significant acceleration for new use cases. However, they always require thoughtful adaptation to new data sources and consumption patterns.

- The human element remains essential—salespeople's knowledge is invaluable data that must be systematically captured through properly incentivized CRM practices.

- Integration across disparate data sources (CRM, website analytics, external data feeds, preference tracking) is what transforms isolated insights into actionable intelligence that can drive specific business outcomes.

For organizations embarking on similar journeys, the path to success requires striking a balance between ambition and pragmatism. Start with a focused business case, such as BestPlatform's "right customer" identification, and build the necessary data and organizational capabilities. Then, systematically expand to address adjacent challenges, like channel optimization.

Case Study 3: Customer Lifetime Value

One of the most powerful mindset shifts modern businesses can adopt is moving from a transactional view of customers to a relationship-oriented perspective. At the heart of this transformation is the concept of **Customer Lifetime Value (CLV).**

What do we mean by customer lifetime value?

Customer Lifetime Value (CLV) represents the total revenue a business can reasonably expect to generate from a single customer throughout their entire relationship. This metric goes beyond measuring immediate transactions to encapsulate the complete economic value of establishing and nurturing customer relationships.

Strategic Importance for Growth

This perspective shift from short-term transactions to long-term relationship building drives several growth mechanisms. See Figure 7.

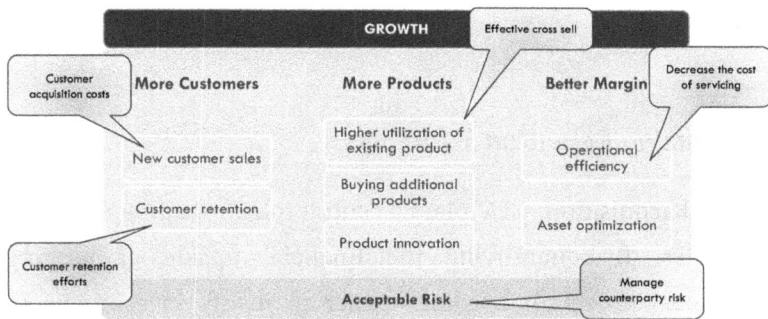

Figure 7: Customer Lifetime Value (CLV) is the total amount of money a customer is expected to spend with a business during the lifetime of an average business relationship.

Driving Efficient Customer Acquisition

Understanding CLV enables companies to make more informed decisions about how much to invest in acquiring new customers. Without a clear view of a customer's long-term value, organizations risk two common pitfalls. On one hand, they may underspend on customer acquisition, missing out on viable growth opportunities by being too conservative. On the other hand, they may overspend, pursuing aggressive marketing tactics that are ultimately unsustainable.

The relationship between CLV and Customer Acquisition Cost (CAC) becomes a key performance indicator in this context. A commonly cited benchmark is a CLV:CAC ratio of 3:1 or better, indicating that for every dollar spent acquiring a customer, the business earns three dollars over the lifetime of that relationship. Maintaining this balance is essential for scaling efficiently and sustainably.

Optimizing Retention Strategies

Beyond acquisition, CLV plays a central role in shaping retention strategies. By quantifying the financial upside of keeping customers longer, it becomes easier to justify investments in customer experience, loyalty programs, and personalized engagement.

The impact of retention is multifold. Extending customer relationships not only boosts individual CLV but also reduces churn, lowers acquisition pressure, and fosters advocacy. Loyal customers become brand ambassadors, referring others and creating a network effect that further enhances growth. CLV provides the metrics needed to prioritize these efforts and measure their ROI.

Informing Product and Service Development

CLV also brings valuable clarity to product development. By analyzing which products and services are most associated with long, profitable customer relationships, companies can align their product roadmaps accordingly. This insight helps prioritize features that enhance stickiness, drive repeat usage, or solve key pain points.

Furthermore, CLV analytics enable smarter bundling and pricing strategies, allowing businesses to tailor their offerings to maximize customer engagement and lifetime profitability. Rather than guessing which features or combinations add the most value, organizations can rely on data to guide these decisions.

Enhancing Operational Efficiency

While CLV is often seen as a revenue metric, it is equally about profitability. Maximizing a customer's lifetime value means not only increasing what they spend but also optimizing the costs associated with serving them.

Operational efficiency is therefore a critical lever in the CLV equation. Reducing the cost of service delivery, whether through automation, better onboarding, self-service options, or improved customer support, can significantly enhance profitability. However, this must be done carefully: striking the right balance between customer experience and cost-to-serve is a delicate art, and one where data and analytics can provide a powerful competitive edge.

What do companies need to know to be able to calculate CLV?

Client revenue: the amount of money the client pays for products and services and any additional fees. For example, for a credit card, the major revenue stream consists of the merchants' fees the credit card issuer receives with every purchase. There is also an additional revenue stream based on fees that are charged to the cardholder: late payment fees, over-the-limit fees, foreign transaction fees, etc.

Client revenue is usually a relatively straightforward calculation when done separately for each of the product/business lines. However, having a full view of all of the revenues generated by a customer is often a challenge in companies with multiple business or product lines. Let me give you an example from my own experience as a bank customer.

This bank was well-known in the industry for its effective use of data in its credit card business. But I wasn't their credit card customer, I had a checking account and an investment account with the part of the bank they had acquired relatively recently. On the banking side, they were really pushing an e-delivery of statements, and I agreed. I hated all the useless paper accumulating in my home, especially as I moved from a large suburban house to an apartment in the city. They had faithfully promised that all my statements would be available to me within

48 hours. Of course, a couple of years later, I needed these statements going back two years. I duly requested the electronic version and received a very surprising note: I can have 6 months' worth of statements for free, but any statements further back would cost me $10 each. Wow! I had a non-trivial amount of money sitting in the investment account with a different business line, and here they were nickel-and-diming me for my own data. I called the customer service to point that out, and no dice—the rep had no visibility into any other accounts I had with this bank and couldn't help at all. Their credit card business was data-driven, but not the rest of the bank. I stopped being both their banking and investment management customer soon afterward, though I still have their credit cards.

This challenge often gives rise to enterprise-wide Client 360 efforts—the very first use case being a 360-degree view of the client's revenues.

Client costs: When evaluating the long-term value of a customer, it is not enough to consider revenue alone. Equally important is the cost to serve, that is, the total expense incurred to continue delivering products or services to a client throughout the duration of the relationship. These costs can vary widely depending on the industry, business model, and delivery mechanism. Still, they all share a common purpose: maintaining the ability to reliably and efficiently fulfill customer needs.

Let us examine what "cost to serve" looks like across various industries, with specific examples that highlight the nature of these ongoing operational expenses.

- **Manufacturing**: In the manufacturing sector, particularly in consumer electronics, one of the most significant costs is associated with sourcing raw materials and components. Companies must procure metals, plastics, semiconductors, and other specialized parts required to assemble the final product. These are direct input costs that are scaled in proportion to production volume. As demand increases, the financial outlay needed to maintain a consistent level of output also increases.

- **Software-as-a-Service (SaaS)**: In SaaS businesses, the cost to serve is largely tied to cloud infrastructure and platform hosting. Maintaining service availability requires continuous investment in cloud services such as Amazon Web Services (AWS), Microsoft Azure, or Google Cloud. These platforms charge for server uptime, data storage, bandwidth, and API calls. As the user base grows, these costs can scale rapidly, making infrastructure planning and optimization critical to maintaining healthy margins.

- **Retail**: In retail, particularly in the apparel industry, the cost to serve revolves around inventory management and logistics. Companies must invest in warehouse space, inventory tracking systems, and the physical transportation of goods—either to brick-and-mortar locations or directly to consumers. These costs are dynamic and sensitive to seasonality, demand variability, and global supply chain disruptions.

- **Healthcare**: In the healthcare sector, outpatient clinics must consider the costs associated with the utilization of medical personnel and equipment. This includes salaries for doctors, nurses, and technicians, as well as ongoing expenses related to diagnostic machines, treatment tools, and clinical software systems. In many cases, medical equipment is leased or depreciated over time, resulting in a recurring financial obligation even after the initial acquisition.

- **Financial services**: In financial services, and particularly in consumer banking, the cost to serve encompasses a range of customer support and compliance operations. Banks must maintain call centers, fraud prevention units, and Know Your Customer (KYC) teams. Additionally, they invest in regulatory compliance systems to meet local and international legal requirements. These processes, while non-revenue generating, are essential for maintaining trust and operational continuity.

Each of these types of companies would have many additional costs beyond the examples I gave.

Client costs are a more difficult part of calculating CLV. While it seems easy for product manufacturing companies to understand the cost of a specific product the client has (for instance, the cost of manufacturing a smartphone), it's usually much harder to allocate the cost of customer service to each client. It's intuitively obvious that if a client is "high maintenance"—that is, requires a lot of hand-holding and support yet doesn't upgrade or acquire a new version of the product, that client would have a lower CLV and perhaps not be a good candidate for generous retention offers. However, collecting this data and connecting it to the client's revenue to inform retention offers in real time is complex.

To illustrate, let me once again use an example from my personal experience as a cable company customer. This was quite a few years back, I've "cut the cord" a long time ago, but I still remember being able to call my cable company every time they proposed a rate increase and avoid the increase by threatening to drop their service. Surprisingly, even though they had a monopoly on cable service in my area of Manhattan and most buildings, including mine, did not allow installation of satellite dishes, it worked more often than not—I would get out of having to pay a higher rate. By the time they wised up and stopped offering retention bonuses to me (I was not a high CLV customer—I didn't pay for premium channels, I never ordered pay-per-view, I had just slightly more than the basic cable), Roku and other "cut the cord" services came along. I dropped my cable service and never came back. The moral of this story is that retention efforts should be closely tied to a customer's LTV, not to mention the availability, quality, and pricing of competitors' products.

Another challenge in understanding the clients' costs is that for many companies that sell services rather than products, the cost of each service is often difficult to calculate. For example, what is the basic cost of a checking account to the bank? Cost of the systems, customer service, and compliance? Is that lower or higher than the cost of a credit card account? Should the bank treat its checking account customers the same as credit card customers? I've worked in a couple of banks, and yet I would struggle to answer these questions definitively based on my general understanding of the business. What's needed is data, well-organized and easily allocated to the right products and services.

Current client tenure: the amount of time a customer maintains a relationship with the company.

While this is the easiest driver of CLV so far, it's not as easy as it seems.

First, "maintains a relationship" is open to different interpretations. Here are some likely ones:

- Is it the number of years since the first time this entity became a customer?

- Or is it the most recent time?

To illustrate, I used to be a Verizon FIOS customer back when I had a house in the suburbs. Then I moved to the city and my apartment building didn't have it, so I used something else, and then, oh joy, it arrived and I became a customer again. Should my tenure with Verizon be counted from the very first time they got FIOS into my home, or just the most recent one? Reasonable people can disagree, and both definitions can be right depending on what answers the business is looking for. That's where data governance becomes particularly useful: bringing stakeholders together to define key terms and creating an easily accessible resource to find definitions is one of the primary responsibilities of data governance.

Second, similarly to the client revenue challenge, if an entity is a customer of multiple business lines, in most organizations this information is so siloed that one business line has no visibility into the length of tenure the customer has with another business line and can make retention mistakes that would have a much broader impact than their own set of products.

Projected client tenure. Projected client tenure is a forward-looking metric that estimates how long a customer is expected to stay with a company, based on current data and trends. One variable in this calculation is an internal piece of data: that is, the term specified in the customer contract. It can vary from terminating at will (for instance, the majority of consumer products and services) to a set period of time with early termination penalties and pre-negotiated terms of renewal.

Other factors are external trends, such as average tenure for customers of similar products, prior history of this specific customer with your company, or with your type of product or service.

To make this a little bit more real, let's look at the example of a technology consulting company trying to estimate the projected client tenure for its biggest client. As you can imagine, this is a crucial number to get right. A lot depends on it, from resource hiring and retention, to investments in training and upskilling to potential expansion and acquisition plans. So, how would a consulting company go about evaluating the projected tenure of its largest client?

First, it would be necessary to get together the current engagements' information. These engagements could be open-ended, time-and-material engagements, or they could be fixed-time/fixed-cost engagements. Both have associated end dates, but time-and-material engagements are more prone to ending with as little as two weeks' notice, while fixed-cost engagements are much more likely to run the specified length of time. This means that the analytical model that's calculating this value would have to treat these contracts differently.

Second, the consulting company can look at its own history with this client:

- How often and how readily have the engagements been renewed?

- Are there new competitors that have signed services agreements with this client that can siphon off the new engagements?

- Has there been a leadership change? Quite often, new leaders have their own vendors they have worked with previously, and they move work their way—I have certainly done that.

- Is the client happy with the work that's been completed recently?

How would the company even know the answers to these questions in the form of data that can be pulled into the analytical model? The most common way is a thoughtful, well-designed, and consistent use of the CRM system by the main point of contact for this client. Similar to our discussion in the data-driven distribution business case earlier, data governance and making data quality of CRM data a key responsibility of client-facing personnel is invaluable here.

An additional factor that would drive the projected tenure calculation would be external trends for the customers of your type of product or service in your industry. These would come from outside vendors and would have to be combined with the rest of the internal information to produce the projected tenure estimate.

To recap, the major drivers of CLV are:

- **Client revenue:** The sum of all revenue a customer generates across all product lines. This can be hard to measure if company data is siloed.

- **Client costs:** Expenses tied to serving the customer (for instance, support, infrastructure). High-maintenance, low-revenue customers would have much lower CLVs. Keep in mind that understanding cost allocation is especially hard in service-based businesses.

- **Client tenure:** The length of time a customer has been with the company. Tenure can be tricky to define and track across business units without clear data governance.

- **Projected client tenure:** An estimate of how long a client will stay based on contracts, engagement history, satisfaction, and market trends. Requires strong CRM usage and reliable internal/external data to model accurately.

Figure 8 shows the Customer Lifetime Value information map.

Now that we have discussed what kind of information or data is needed to calculate CLV, let's talk about the data capabilities required to do it consistently, correctly, and automatically. For any company in any industry, having a comprehensive view of its customers and their journeys, from customer acquisition and onboarding, to product and service operations, and on to customer offboarding, across all business lines, is essential.

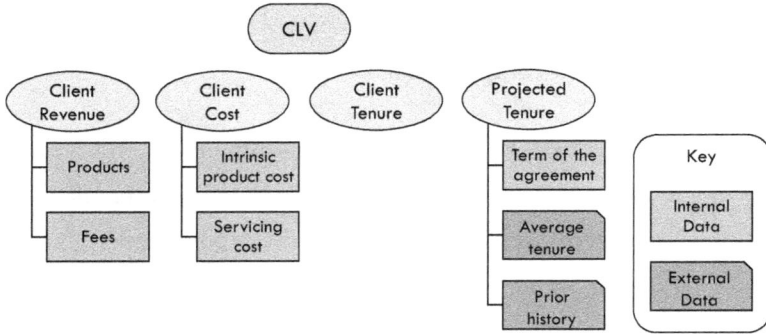

Figure 8: Customer lifetime value–generic.

Master data management for both customers and products becomes particularly critical in CLV contexts because the accurate lifetime value calculations depend on creating unified, longitudinal views of customer interactions and product consumption patterns. Customer MDM must resolve identity across multiple touchpoints and systems to ensure revenue attribution accuracy, while product MDM enables maintaining consistent cost structures and profitability metrics that feed directly into CLV calculations. Without proper MDM, CLV models risk double-counting revenues, misattributing customer behaviors, or applying incorrect cost assumptions that can dramatically skew lifetime value predictions.

Data governance takes on heightened importance for CLV initiatives because these calculations often span multiple business units and require consistent definitions of key metrics like customer acquisition costs, retention rates, and churn indicators. CRM data ownership becomes especially crucial since customer relationship data forms the backbone of behavioral modeling in CLV algorithms. The governance framework must establish clear accountability for data quality metrics that directly impact CLV accuracy—such as transaction completeness, customer status consistency, and product information integrity. Additionally, as in previous case studies, understanding and managing reliable sources of both internal and external data is necessary for accurate and actionable CLV, particularly when incorporating market benchmarks, competitive intelligence, or economic indicators that influence customer behavior patterns and lifetime value projections.

The Case of Best Cell Inc.

To demonstrate how Customer Lifetime Value (CLV) can serve as a foundation for a customer retention strategy, consider the case of BestCell Inc., a fictitious name used to protect confidentiality. BestCell offers both mobile and Wi-Fi services to individual consumers, and also sells mobile devices, although purchasing a device from BestCell is optional for customers. While hardware sales contribute to revenue, the company's core business model revolves around subscription services.

In this case study, BestCell's strategic objective was to consistently and accurately identify the highest-value customers at risk of churning and to surface this information in a timely, actionable manner, making it available to any customer service representative at any point of contact. Achieving this required answering two critical questions: "Who are the most valuable customers?" and "When are they at risk of leaving?"

The first question was fundamentally a CLV challenge. BestCell defined their most valuable customers as those with the highest projected lifetime value over the duration of their relationship with the company, going beyond the "highest monthly bills today" definition. Identifying these customers necessitated a nuanced understanding of both revenue and cost over time.

Understanding Customer Revenue

Revenue, of course, was the starting point. In BestCell's case, revenue could be generated through several channels, including mobile subscription plans, Wi-Fi services, and the sale or financing of mobile devices. However, the complexity resided in the fact that each of these revenue streams was managed through separate systems. To assemble a complete picture of a customer's contribution, BestCell had to consolidate this data into a single, cohesive view.

This included tracking base subscription fees, fees from optional add-ons such as international calling, roaming, or enhanced technical support, as well as income from device sales. But historical revenue alone was not sufficient. To predict future value, BestCell needed to understand the customer's growth potential, such as whether the customer is using both mobile and

Wi-Fi services, or only one. If a mobile customer lived in an area where Wi-Fi is also available, that customer represented an opportunity for cross-selling.

Additionally, historical behavioral patterns offered important clues. A customer who has previously switched between providers and returned may present a less stable, risk-prone profile. In contrast, a consistently engaged customer is more likely to be retained with minimal effort.

To make sense of these disparate signals, BestCell required a strong foundation of data capabilities. Here we came across our old friends: data governance and master data management. Defining consistent sources of truth across systems (data governance) was essential to ensure that the data used in decision-making is reliable. Equally important was the ability to link customer information across different business units, which would be enabled by master data management. Without these capabilities, BestCell couldn't accurately identify which services or purchases belong to which customer, limiting the usefulness of any CLV analysis.

Understanding Customer Cost

While revenue is one side of the CLV equation, understanding customer-level cost is equally critical. BestCell had to continually assess the cost of delivering each service a customer received, which included both the direct costs of service delivery and the indirect costs associated with maintaining the customer relationship.

For BestCell, this involved charges paid to other carriers when customers use roaming or interconnection services. Device costs, such as those tied to subsidized phone purchases or upgrade programs, also contributed to the overall expense.

Customer support costs varied widely. Some customers placed frequent calls to support centers or required extended troubleshooting, which demanded a disproportionate amount of time and resources. Others churned frequently, incurring costs during both the offboarding and re-onboarding processes. Additionally, the financial impact of retention incentives had to be considered. Loyalty programs, discounts, and free upgrades, while increasing retention, also represented tangible costs that affected profitability.

Administrative functions, such as billing, fraud prevention, and managing unpaid accounts, constituted another layer of operational expenses. Taken together, these costs helped determine how much it took to serve a customer over time, and whether that service relationship was truly sustainable.

For BestCell, the primary additional data capability to understand costs was establishing product and service master data management, that is, having a centralized repository of well-defined products and services connected to all product-related systems end-to-end.

Calculating Customer Tenure

Customer tenure was relatively easy to obtain in a company with just two product lines, as long as start and end dates are collected, saved, and associated with the customer ID. Master data management of customer data was the primary data capability required to make customer tenure available for calculating CLV and addressing the retention challenge.

Predicting Projected Customer Tenure

While calculating current tenure was relatively easy, calculating the projected tenure became a much more complex exercise. Here is the information BestCell needed to know to accomplish that:

- **Type of contract**: Post-paid contracts, especially with device financing, have a natural lock-in. Prepaid customers, on the other hand, can churn instantly. This would seem simple enough information to get, after all, BestCell had to have this information on hand to bill the customer appropriately. However, its billing systems were rudimentary and did not have all the contract's "small print" codified. From the data management capabilities perspective, it presented two options for BestCell: extending data governance to the billing systems or using GenAI to parse out contracts and make the information available for retention analytics. While generally speaking, this was not a bad use case for GenAI, given how new this technology was and how uncertain the costs were, BestCell had to be careful not to have its methods of calculating CLV decrease the actual CLV. Additionally, going directly to the contract documentation invites another data management capability in: records management. After all, to have accurate analytics, BestCell would want to refer to the latest document, not the one from the previous service renewal.

- **Customer tenure history**: Customers who have been with the company the longest are most likely to stay.

- **Plan type and usage**: Customers who have a bundle of both cell and Wi-Fi services were more likely to stay with the service longer. Similarly, customers of family plans faced a similar issue, as switching in either case would be more of a hassle. Customers of just cell services were likelier to switch than Wi-Fi service customers, since, again, it's usually more of a hassle to switch Wi-Fi versus cell service.

- **Device lifecycle timing**: This was the other side of postpaid contracts with the device financing included— tenure often aligned with the device lifecycle.

- **Demographic factors**: For example, age seems to correlate with loyalty; that is, younger customers switch more often.

Figure 9 shows the Top Clients at Risk information map for BestCell.

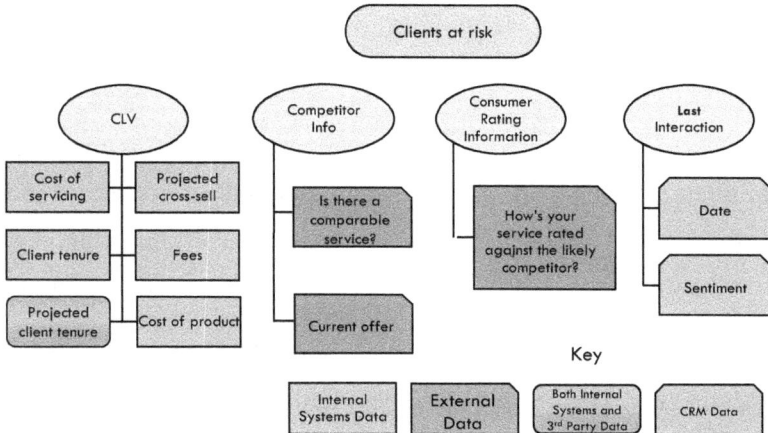

Figure 9: Telecommunications: client retention. The goal is to identify top clients at risk.

Operationalizing CLV at BestCell

To realize value from this effort and put it into practice, BestCell had to go beyond one-off analysis. BestCell's end-state vision was to enable any customer-facing employee to take effective actions if a high-value customer showed signs of dissatisfaction, perhaps through a spike in support calls or a sudden drop in usage. There were three goals for intervention: it had to be timely, relevant to the customer, and aligned with the customer value.

To achieve this vision, BestCell built a roadmap to develop a reporting and analytics platform that continuously tracked and updated CLV metrics, integrated them into frontline systems, and empowered customer-facing teams to act accordingly.

What are the data capabilities BestCell needs to leverage to operationalize this vision?

In addition to extending data governance beyond customer operations teams and systems to product and service teams and systems, and Master Data Management beyond customer information to product information, data collection became of paramount importance.

Thorough data collection is a data management discipline that doesn't receive enough attention, but it really ought to. Business lines do well when collecting data to support their immediate operations. However, when it comes to collecting information that's needed for analytics, it's often an afterthought. For example, while call centers typically collect information about the length of calls and the most common questions asked, they often do not automatically collect and save the information that identifies the customer, connecting it to the call's length and purpose.

What about data quality? Let's assume for a moment that BestCell has already established an analytical data environment to accelerate its sales process and has essentially implemented our previous sales acceleration case study. For that case study, the majority of the data came from either external sources or the CRM, and the data quality measurement (DQM) was implemented in the analytical environment, as BestCell couldn't directly measure data quality at the source for the external data. However, for this case study, the calculation of CLV primarily relied on data from internal transaction systems. Implementing the DQM discipline after the data is pulled into the analytical environment and either fixing it there or using the Issue Management and Resolution (IMR) process to find root causes in the source systems and fix them there, would leverage the data quality capabilities previously established. However, this "after the fact" approach was expensive and thus reduced the customer lifetime value the company was aiming to maximize. A more cost-effective and thus higher value approach was to establish data quality by design, by, for example, assigning common IDs to new customers as they are onboarded, by standardizing reference data such as zip codes and address information, and by putting controls, both programmatic and operational, at the time of data creation. One of the major challenges data teams face is the resistance of front office teams to prioritize "data quality by design" changes in the absence of immediate impact on their day-to-day operations. What we found in BestCell was that tying it to their retention goals and showing direct correspondence between better CLV (that is, better profits) and better retention made it much easier to get over that challenge.

Now that we know who BestCell's top customers are, let's turn our attention to what's needed to identify which of them are at risk and what the next best action is to retain them.

How would BestCell know that?

It would need to look at the external factors and the most recent interaction history. Let's take it one step at a time.

First, who were the competitors?

- Is there a comparable service? In other words, is BestCell the only game in town for either of its services? That would be highly unlikely in the case of cell service, at least in the US. However, Wi-Fi service providers were much scarcer, even in highly urbanized areas, until recently.

- If there is a viable competitor, are they running any current promotions that could entice away BestCell's top customers?

Second, how well did BestCell stack up to these competitors? What were the official rankings by Consumer Reports and other similar publications? What was the prevailing local sentiment as judged by Yelp and TikTok reviews?

Third, were there any signals that your top customers were getting unhappy? How was the last interaction? Have they been calling the service center more frequently than usual, and what was the tone of these phone calls? What were the calls about? Were they about a new and exciting product BestCell has just launched, or about issues with their existing services?

For the first two aspects, BestCell would have to acquire this information from data brokers. The third was based on internal information, and it emphasized once again the importance of thorough and thoughtful (and ethical!) data collection at all customer touchpoints.

To summarize, BestCell needed to establish these capabilities to understand who its top customers are:

- Data governance
- Master data management for customer, product, and services data
- Records management
- Detailed data collection of behavior and usage
- AI—GenAI to make contract information available for analytics and for the last mile insights delivery, Machine Learning (ML) for predictive analysis of project client tenure

Here are the key takeaways from this case study:

- **Retention requires external and internal interaction data**: Identifying at-risk top customers involves monitoring competitor activity, external sentiment, and internal customer interaction signals, highlighting the need for ethical, comprehensive customer data capture.

- **Revenue and cost data must be integrated**: Companies need unified data on customer revenue (across services, devices, add-ons) and costs (service delivery, support, churn, billing, etc.) to assess CLV effectively.

- **Tenure and contract insights drive predictive CLV:** Understanding current and projected customer tenure through contract types, usage patterns, device cycles, and demographics requires clean, connected data across systems.

- **Robust data management at the source is critical:** The goal of "Top Clients at Risk" reporting and analytics is to increase the company's profitability by identifying which of their top clients are at risk and extending their tenure and thus their lifetime value. But if this reporting is manually driven, requiring extensive mapping and data corrections, the effort to produce it would eat into the CLV it's trying to increase. An accurate, consistent, and automated CLV calculation requires comprehensive data governance, source systems integration with master data management for customers and products, disciplined, analytics-focused data collection, and last but not least, data quality management at the source, i.e., data quality by design.

Case Study 4: Data Monetization

What is data monetization? Here is a definition from Gartner:

Data Monetization refers to the process of using data to obtain quantifiable economic benefits. Internal or indirect methods include using data to make measurable improvements in business performance and decisions. External or direct methods include data sharing to gain beneficial terms or conditions from business partners, information bartering, selling data outright (via a data broker or independently), or offering information products and services (for example, including information as a value-added component of an existing offering).

This is a very broad definition that is closely aligned with the definition I offered earlier in this book, which involves using data for offense, specifically to generate more revenue. In this case study, I aim to explore a specific type of data monetization: leveraging information from an existing business line(s) to create a completely new set of products or services. Eventually, this new set of products may become a whole new business line for the company.

This type of data monetization is especially important for companies that have a major business line generating the highest revenue but suffering from small and continually shrinking margins. In other words, while it's still generating revenues, the cost to do so is rising, and profitability is eroding. The result is an unsustainable trajectory where volume masks underlying financial fragility. This problem affects both new, tech-native firms and older, asset-heavy incumbents across industries. Unfortunately, there is no easy button for solving this challenge. Using data from this core business to build something new offers one path, which still isn't easy but has fewer risks for the revenue-producing core.

Here are some industry examples to make this challenge more concrete:

- **Amazon**: Amazon's e-commerce operation is a global revenue engine, but the profit margins in that business are notoriously slim. Costs associated with warehousing, logistics, and relentless price competition erode earnings. Yet, Amazon has leveraged its infrastructure and behavioral data to form the foundation for its higher-margin and fast-growing advertising business. This newer unit accounted for a disproportionate share of Amazon's profits, and it was built from insights and capabilities created in retail.

- **Netflix**: Netflix still earns most of its revenue through direct subscriptions, but that model is under pressure. The cost of content continues to rise, and subscriber growth is flattening in key markets. In response, Netflix is exploring higher-margin alternatives, such as licensing its original content to third parties and rolling out ad-supported tiers. Both approaches monetize existing assets more efficiently than traditional subscriptions.

- **Uber**: Uber has faced the harsh economics of its core rideshare business. Though mobility services generate most of its revenue, the margins are undercut by driver incentives, insurance costs, and regulatory constraints. To combat this, Uber has expanded into areas where its existing data, infrastructure, and customer relationships give it a strategic edge, such as freight logistics, advertising placements, and food delivery via Uber Eats, which offer potentially stronger margins. Again, these expansions leverage the data and capabilities of its core mobility platform.

- **General Motors**: GM's mass-market sedans sell in volume, but demand is shifting, and the segment suffers from intense price competition. Meanwhile, the company's financing and leasing services generate significantly higher margins. GM is also using vehicle usage data and driver behavior analytics to inform its push into electric vehicles and subscription-based features—another form of data-driven monetization.

The really challenging part of this situation is that there isn't very much a company can do in its core business to fix this problem. They can't sell their biggest business—what would Amazon be without its e-tail or Uber without the rides? And there is only so much efficiency you can squeeze from your own operations and technology. Moreover, a majority of the margin compression is often due to external factors.

So, what can you do? One of the approaches is to use the relationships and the data the company obtains from its big, but margin-challenged, business line and create a new set of products and services that can command higher margins.

Some of the examples above demonstrate that approach:

- Advertising revenue for Amazon takes advantage of the enormous amount of data Amazon has on its customers and vendors.

- Financing services for GM are offered to the buyers of its cars, leveraging the relationships from the legacy business line.

For this case study, we will go back to the financial services industry by looking at how BestRetire (a composite of several retirement services companies), can solve its "high revenue, low margin" challenge.

The retirement services industry in the U.S., particularly the 401(k)-recordkeeping sector, is a textbook example of a high-revenue, low-margin business under pressure to transform.

First, let's set the industry context.

In the United States, retirement is, for the most part, an individual responsibility. Unlike countries with universal pension systems, the U.S. retirement model is a fragmented patchwork that relies heavily on employer-sponsored plans, private savings, and Social Security. A crucial feature of this system is the tax treatment of retirement savings: the U.S. Internal Revenue Code allows individuals to set aside pre-tax income for retirement through tax-advantaged accounts, such as 401(k) plans, traditional IRAs, and other qualified retirement plans. These incentives form the bedrock of the defined contribution retirement system.

To understand how we got here, it's essential to differentiate between the two major paradigms of retirement planning: defined benefit (DB) and defined contribution (DC) plans.

- Defined Benefit (DB) Plans (commonly referred to as pensions) guarantee employees a fixed monthly income in retirement, based on factors like salary history and years of service. These plans were dominant in the mid-20th century, especially in unionized industries and the public sector. In a DB plan, the employer bears the investment risk and is responsible for funding any shortfall. Over time, many private-sector employers phased out DB plans due to the long-term liabilities and volatility they introduced to corporate balance sheets.

- Defined Contribution (DC) Plans, by contrast, shift the burden of saving and investing to the employee. The most common form, the 401(k), allows employees to contribute a portion of their paycheck into a retirement account, often with an employer match. The employee chooses how to invest those contributions, typically from a menu of mutual funds, and the final retirement benefit depends on market performance and individual contribution behavior. Employers bear significantly less financial risk under this model, which has contributed to its widespread adoption.

Today, the vast majority of private-sector workers with retirement benefits participate in defined contribution plans. Public sector workers still often receive defined benefit pensions, though many of these systems are under fiscal strain.

However, the defined contribution system creates a new set of complexities. Because each employee's account must be individually tracked, invested, reported on, and administered, the operational infrastructure behind these plans is significant. This has given rise to a specialized industry: recordkeeping.

The Recordkeeping Function and Margin Squeeze

What is a recordkeeper?

It's a company that manages the administrative and technical machinery behind employer-sponsored retirement plans. Recordkeepers are responsible for tracking contributions and balances, processing distributions, maintaining compliance with IRS and Department of Labor regulations, providing online portals for participants, and communicating plan-related information to both employers and employees.

Despite the complexity and importance of this role, the recordkeeping business has become brutally margin-compressed. Fees have declined steeply over the past decade due to increased competition, commoditization, and regulatory scrutiny over hidden costs. In a world where every basis point (0.01%) of cost is scrutinized, many recordkeepers find themselves managing massive operational workloads for increasingly lower compensation.

To make matters worse, many of the industry's largest incumbents still rely on legacy systems and outdated processes, such as Excel-based manual workflows or inflexible mainframe platforms. These systems were built for a different era and now hinder innovation, increase operational risk, and raise the cost of doing business.

On the plus side, the recordkeepers operate in a stakeholder-rich ecosystem, creating multiple strong relationships.

Who are the most important stakeholders?

1. Plan Sponsor (The Employer)

The plan sponsor is the employer that offers the retirement benefit to its employees. This entity is the legal and contractual customer of the recordkeeper. Plan sponsors can range from small businesses with fewer than 50 employees to Fortune 500 multinational corporations with tens of thousands of workers.

For plan sponsors, offering a 401(k) plan is both a recruiting and retention tool, and a compliance responsibility. Sponsors are required to adhere to a range of fiduciary and administrative obligations under ERISA (Employee Retirement Income Security Act), including ensuring that plan fees are reasonable, investment options are appropriate, and participant communications are clear and accurate.

Most sponsors lack internal expertise or infrastructure to manage these obligations directly. As a result, they outsource recordkeeping, investment lineup design, and even fiduciary oversight to third parties. However, sponsors are still legally on the hook as fiduciaries, which makes vendor selection a high-stakes decision.

Cost is a major concern for sponsors, especially in an environment where benefit budgets are tight and plan participants expect consumer-grade digital experiences. At the same time, sponsors want their employees to be financially secure in retirement, which places pressure on them to go beyond the bare minimum in plan design.

2. Plan Participant (The Employee)

The plan participant is the individual employee who contributes to and benefits from the retirement plan. This group is the end user of the record-keeping system and associated financial services.

Participants vary widely in age, income, financial literacy, and investment experience. A 22-year-old new hire may need educational tools to understand compound interest, while a 63-year-old nearing retirement may need sophisticated drawdown strategies or annuity options.

Participants interact with the retirement system through web portals, mobile apps, call centers, and plan communications. Their experience with these tools has a significant impact on their satisfaction with the plan, and, by extension, their employer.

Importantly, participants are increasingly seen as a target market for cross-selling. Many recordkeepers and plan advisors aim to convert participants into individual wealth management clients when they change jobs or retire—this is where margins are much higher.

3. Plan Advisor (The Intermediary)

Plan advisors, also known as retirement plan consultants, play a crucial role as intermediaries between plan sponsors and the retirement services industry. Their primary role is to assist employers in designing, implementing, and managing their retirement plans.

Advisors help sponsors:

- Select a recordkeeper
- Design the investment lineup
- Ensure compliance with fiduciary rules
- Benchmark fees and services
- Educate participants on retirement planning.

Plan advisors can work independently or as part of larger wealth management firms. They often straddle the line between institutional and retail services, offering financial planning to individuals in addition to advising corporations.

This dual role creates both opportunities and conflicts. On one hand, advisors are well-positioned to help participants with rollovers, IRAs, and post-retirement income planning. On the other hand, their compensation models and fiduciary obligations are under growing scrutiny, especially when participants are "cross-sold" products that may or may not be in their best interest.

This foundational structure—plan sponsor, plan participant, and plan advisor—is what the recordkeeper must manage, support, enable, and ideally utilize to create more profitable products and services, as well as new business lines.

Now that we have a better understanding of the retirement industry context, let's examine what BestRetire aimed to achieve with its monetization strategy.

BestRetire has been experiencing all the challenges of the industry:

- Its operations are largely manual.

- Technology infrastructure is based on a more than 20-year-old set of systems that are inflexible, badly documented, and resistant to change.

- While it often wins very large deals with top employers in the US, the margins are getting smaller and smaller with each win.

- It has already gone through multiple efforts to reduce the operating costs, and while further reductions are possible, BestRetire cannot solve this challenge by cost reductions alone.

Over the last few years, BestRetire had been investing in modern data and digital capabilities and its business strategies aimed to leverage these capabilities, the enormous amount of data it had, and the relationships it had built with the advisors to create a new set of products aimed at the advisors who also offer retail services: providing them with the likely prospects for their services.

Thus, the goal of this case study is to identify the best prospects for retail financial services.

What information would BestRetire need to be able to create this product?

First, it would need to bring together the information it has about all the participants it serves. BestRetire possessed a wealth of incredibly valuable information about participants, including their personal details such as age, name, contact information, years of service at the current company, income, current investment portfolio, and even household members. While this information was important, advisors could also obtain it from external brokers. Therefore, while it was beneficial that BestRetire had this information at its fingertips, it wasn't a significant differentiator. What was a differentiator, though, was the information about participants' behavior as it related to their investment portfolio. Were they on top of it? How often did they check their position? What did they do when the market fell? Did they buy more stock, or did they flee into the bonds or cash? In other words, BestRetire had information that indicated a participant's level of sophistication and risk tolerance. This knowledge, combined with age, income, and household information, offered genuine differentiation.

What were the capabilities needed to bring this information together automatically and correctly? As always, data governance, data quality, and master data management were important—age and transaction history, for example, usually reside in different systems, and a) these systems needed to be identified (aka governed) and b) connected to the same participant (aka master data management (MDM)). Here I'd like to emphasize again the difference between data and data capability. As I mentioned, BestRetire had been investing in data capabilities, including Data Governance and MDM. The data governance and data quality capabilities built to date were fully leverageable, that is, there were already data stewards established for the participants' data, authoritative sources identified, and DQ rules and measurement established on this data and these sources. However, while the MDM platform had been implemented and deployed in production, its scope was limited to legal entities (for instance, sponsors). This meant that while a significant portion of the MDM work done so far was leverageable, there was significant new work that would need to be done to bring participants into the MDM platform and, even more importantly, incorporate the golden records back into the source system.

Additionally, a significant new set of data needed to be collected: the behavioral data. While this data was necessary for the monetization strategy, it was not necessary for record-keeping functionality itself, so it had never been collected, let alone saved and tied to a specific participant and market conditions. Most of this data originated in the company's website, so the scope of data governance would need to be extended to this specific type of data—that is, website usage statistics.

While this was a rich trove of participant data, did BestRetire have the right to use it for cross-selling purposes? This was the question of data rights, and it was not a simple question.

Most plan sponsors place contractual and policy-based limitations on how a recordkeeper can use participant data. These restrictions are typically included in service agreements. They are designed to safeguard employee privacy, maintain ERISA compliance, and prevent the unauthorized use of sensitive information for purposes such as marketing or product solicitation. From the sponsor's perspective, participant data, including income, age, employment status, and investment choices, belongs to the plan and must be handled in a fiduciary context. Sponsors are often wary of vendors leveraging this data to cross-sell unrelated financial products, especially if such activity could reflect poorly on the employer or appear to compromise participant trust. These limitations reflect a broader concern about data ethics and responsibility in employer-sponsored benefit ecosystems.

However, participants themselves retain the right to authorize the use of their personal data independently, provided they give informed and explicit consent. This created an alternate path for BestRetire and affiliated advisors to engage participants outside the constraints of the sponsor's control. If a participant voluntarily opted into additional services, BestRetire could legally and ethically use this data for its new Advisor Cross Sell product line.

Obtaining participants' consent to use their data beyond plan administration effectively addressed the legal and ethical challenges. However, there was a data challenge as well:

How could BestRetire differentiate between the participant data it had obtained from the sponsor to which it had no rights, and the data that participants consented to be used for these purposes? The answer was in a whole new data capability I haven't mentioned so far: metadata management.

Metadata management is a business-driven, technology-enabled discipline that manages data about data, including descriptions, Personally Identifiable Information (PII) designation, lineage, and usage rights.

Metadata management was a key data capability for this case study; it really didn't matter how rich and accurate the participants' data set and AI algorithms were at BestRetire, it could not be used to create a new product if BestRetire couldn't distinguish between the data it had rights to and the data it didn't.

Yet again, this clearly illustrates the first point of this book: data alone is insufficient to drive business growth; data capabilities are necessary to achieve that goal.

What other data was needed to make the product indispensable for the advisors? Information about them, of course. More specifically, information about their services, and, very importantly, the linkage between which advisors were associated with which plans and thus participants, and what legal constraints these sponsors of these plans placed on the advisors.

Figure 10 shows the information map for a prospect-product match.

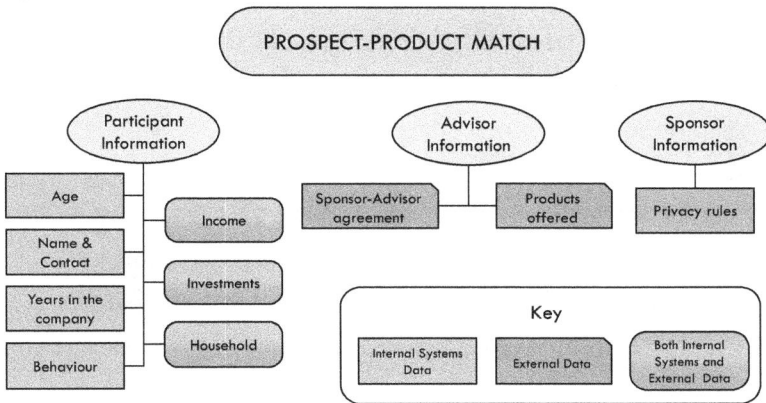

Figure 10: Retirement services to advisor cross-sell. The goal is to identify retail financial services prospects.

To recap:

- **Data monetization as a strategic escape from margin compression**: Many companies operate high-revenue business lines that suffer from shrinking margins due to competition, operational costs, or commoditization. A promising strategy is to monetize data by utilizing it to create entirely new, high-margin products or business lines, leveraging existing assets, such as customer relationships and behavioral insights.

- **Real-world examples of data-driven pivots**: Companies like Amazon, Netflix, Uber, GM, and FedEx all face margin pressure in their core revenue streams. In response, they've leveraged data from those low-margin operations to launch higher-margin adjacent businesses, such as Amazon's advertising, GM's financing services, or Uber's freight and food delivery units.

- **BestRetire use of participant data to enable advisor cross-sell**: BestRetire, a composite of several retirement services companies, operated in a high-revenue, low-margin industry. It aimed to monetize participant data by helping financial advisors identify high-potential retail prospects, based on behavioral and demographic patterns already available in its systems.

- **Data capabilities are the enabler, not just the data itself**: To deliver this new product, BestRetire must unify data across fragmented systems using data governance, master data management, and metadata management. Metadata management is a must-have capability for the monetization strategy, enabling Best Retire to distinguish between data obtained via plan sponsors (with restricted usage rights) and data explicitly consented to by participants, making metadata and data rights tracking essential.

- **Consent and legal use are core to ethical data monetization**: While sponsors restrict how participant data can be used, participants can independently give informed consent for additional services. BestRetire's success hinged on managing data privacy, legal constraints, and consent tracking, while ensuring that any monetization efforts remained compliant and trusted.

Summary

In this chapter, we introduced four business case studies, each one illustrating how different business goals (regulatory compliance, sales acceleration, customer retention, and data monetization) require a combination of data and data capabilities to succeed. Despite different contexts, several core themes emerged across all cases:

1. Business Value Comes from Data + Capability, Not Data Alone

Every case reinforced the core learning of this book: having data isn't enough. Value is unlocked only when organizations have the capabilities, technical, organizational, and process-driven, to make that data usable. For example, in the Risk-Weighted Asset (RWA) case, banks had the data required to meet regulatory requirements. However, without master data management or data quality controls, they were unable to produce consistent or trusted results. The same applied in the sales and marketing case study: BestPlatform had access to rich external and internal data, but it needed MDM and data governance of CRM data to turn that data into the acceleration engine it needed.

2. Reusable Data Capabilities Enable Strategic Scale

A second recurring theme was the reuse of foundational data capabilities across different business goals. Master Data Management (MDM), Data Governance, and Data Quality Management appeared in all four case studies. While the specific data entities, systems, and stewards may differ across use cases, the underlying capabilities were often extensible with adjustments. For instance, the MDM platform built for regulatory compliance in the RWA case can also be leveraged by the sales acceleration use case by bringing in new data sources (like CRM and website traffic) and new consumers (like sales and marketing teams).

3. Operational Efficiency and Margin Growth Depend on Data Quality

Poor data quality is a direct hit to margin and efficiency. In every case, bad or missing data led to costly rework, manual interventions, or over-allocation of resources. For example:

- In the RWA case, missing borrower information led to conservative assumptions and higher capital reserves, reducing lending capacity.

- In the sales acceleration case, inconsistent CRM data slowed down outreach and caused misdirected effort.

- In the CLV/retention case, the absence of unified customer views led to the misidentification of high-value customers and wasted retention spending.

All of these highlight that "data quality by design" at the source is far more scalable and effective than trying to clean data downstream.

4. Data Governance Is a Strategic Enabler, Not Just a Compliance Function

In each case study, governance played a foundational *enabling* role, assigning clear ownership, establishing roles and responsibilities, business operational processes and standards, and ensuring continuity across use cases. In the BestPlatform sales case, governance ensured that external data remained relevant and of high quality over time. In the BestCell customer retention case, governance defined what "customer tenure" meant and ensured consistency across departments. Contrary to the popular view that data governance is a controls check-boxing exercise, these case studies demonstrate that it is a long-term enabler of reuse, adaptability, and value across the enterprise.

5. Organizational Context and Stakeholder Alignment Are Critical

A persistent undercurrent throughout the case studies is that data initiatives fail when business stakeholders don't understand or see the benefits of the data capabilities being proposed. Technical teams may recognize that a Customer 360 platform is crucial for hyper-personalization, but unless it translates into tangible business outcomes (for instance, reducing churn or boosting cross-sell), adoption and support can stall. Success requires not just building capabilities but packaging them in a language and metrics that resonate with business objectives.

6. Strategic Use of Internal + External Data Is a Competitive Advantage

Each case highlights the increasing need to combine internal data with external sources, such as market sentiment, customer behavior, or demographic signals. For instance:

- BestPlatform used external data vendors, analyst call data, and website behavior to refine prospect targeting.

- BestCell utilized internal billing and usage data, alongside competitive offers and social media sentiment, to identify retention risk.

However, this blend only works when external data is governed, monitored, and linked to internal systems through shared keys and effective stewardship.

7. Data Strategy Maturity Enables Compound Returns

As organizations mature in their data capabilities, the effort required to launch new use cases decreases and returns increase.

BestPlatform's second initiative (channel optimization) was faster and easier than the first (identifying the right client), because core capabilities were already in place. The same was true for BestCell: after building out the foundation for CLV, identifying at-risk top clients became an incremental rather than foundational lift. This demonstrates the flywheel effect of data maturity—each investment accelerates the next.

8. Where does AI play a role?

Every single case study we had discussed required the use of AI. For RWA, it was an old-style stochastic modeling of future capital needs across multiple economic scenarios. For sales acceleration, customer retention, and cross-sell monetization case studies, it was multi-pronged:

- Data science predictive models to create the likely prospects list

- GenAI capabilities to simplify CRM data entry for salespeople

- GenAI capabilities to extract value from unstructured document-based data

- GenAI capabilities to deliver insights back to salespeople in the easiest-to-consume format

- And finally, ML and GenAI capabilities to accelerate entity matching and metadata enrichment.

PART TWO

Building the Capability Strategy and Roadmap

In Part 1 of the book, we examined the "why" of data strategy: how to uncover the business value of data for a company and what technical, organizational, and cultural capabilities a company needs to achieve its business goals.

In Part 2, we will get down to the business of building the value-centric roadmap. The first step will be to align the value we have discovered in part 1 across multiple business lines to create a data capability strategy. Then, we will discuss how to evaluate the company's current position, its existing capabilities, and which new ones need to be developed first to achieve its goals. That will help us determine the optimal order in which these capabilities ought to be built. That is, how to create a value-focused roadmap that can deliver on the promise of the flywheel effect of data maturity.

CHAPTER FOUR

Aligning Priorities and Common Capabilities

I began this book by highlighting the danger of focusing data transformation on a single specific goal or initiative. Yet, I then spent the entire first part of the book describing multiple ways to identify such specific goals and value statements. So, a reasonable person can ask: how is my approach different from exactly the trap I cautioned against?

The next step is crucial to avoiding this trap: I call it aligning priorities with the vision and finding common ground.

> To accomplish the first step, **finding value**, you would have had to identify, build relationships, and collaborate with business leaders across the entire company.

As a result of your painstaking work, you now have a robust set of business goals for each of the business lines and for several key enterprise functions, such as finance, marketing, and operations. For each of these goals, you would define which data and data capabilities were needed to achieve them. Returning to our business case study protagonists, if you are at bank, you may have an RWA initiative and also a cross-sell initiative between consumer and small business banking. If you are at BestCell or BestPlatform, you may have sales acceleration and customer retention initiatives. And if you are at BestRetire, you may have profitability insights and advisor cross-sell monetization initiatives on your books. All these initiatives require an overlapping set of data capabilities that must operate on different sets of data and in various business operational and team environments. How do you align all of these needs?

Your next step is to collaborate with all stakeholders to align these initiatives with the company's vision and overall strategy. This is easier said than done, but it's a necessary step to ensure full buy-in and understanding of the data capability strategy and roadmap. To illustrate its importance, let me share another story from my own experience, and it's a cautionary tale. It happened approximately two years into my tenure as a data leader at a financial company. My first set of deliverables was aligned with the corporate financial reporting optimization initiative, which was widely recognized as the company's highest priority.

I was also eager to create value for the business lines and leverage the capabilities my team has built for the finance initiative, thereby showcasing the value of the data work we've been doing so far. I approached two of the company's major business lines. For the first one, we plugged into their project prioritization process and, in multiple meetings, reviewed a complex, multipage spreadsheet to identify a likely initiative for us to take on. And we did find one we can all agree on—way down the list. The initiative sponsor was excited, and we were excited as well—it seemed it would be a clear win once it was delivered. But guess what? It wasn't. I still remember sitting in a meeting with the head of strategy for this business and proudly sharing our achievement and the value I thought we delivered, and her looking at me with genuine puzzlement:

Why did you do this one?
Of all the things you could do, why this one?

And I didn't have a good answer beyond "It seemed like a good idea at the time."

What was my mistake here?

I didn't start in the right place. I didn't start with the overall company's vision. I didn't go to the head of strategy and ask, "What are your priorities and plans to achieve the vision? What is your business strategy?" I had a hammer—the data capabilities we've already built, and I went looking for a nail. I attempted to deliver a strategic win without a clear understanding or connection to the business's vision and strategy.

Did I do better in the second business line? A bit, but not much. I started at the right place: I attended an executive meeting with the head of the business and his direct reports. I went at the right time: at the start of the annual planning process, when the yearly roadmap was defined, before the long spreadsheet of projects was created. But then I asked the wrong question: "What are your data needs that I can help you with by leveraging what we've built for finance?" The pushback was immediate and strong: they didn't have any data needs that the "enterprise" group could help with, and I should return to the finance team to determine my next set of priorities. Keep in mind, I wasn't asking for funding; I was asking how I could help them achieve their goals. But I didn't ask the right question.

What was the right question? Actually, it's not asking one at all at this type of meeting; it's about listening and identifying stakeholders who are responsible for the strategic initiatives. Then, you go to them to understand their goals and immediate priorities and educate them on how data capabilities can accelerate the process. And, very importantly, not doing it alone but in partnership with the head of technology for this business— after all, the head of technology had both a relationship and trust, and enabling success together would have been a much better story for both of us.

I did learn from these mistakes, and a year later, I had strategic initiatives going with these two business lines that a) were fully aligned with vision and strategy and recognized as such; and b) were leveraging the technical and organizational data capabilities that my team has been building.

To illustrate the alignment step, let's examine a new business case study: developing a data strategy and roadmap for a biotechnology startup. To preserve confidentiality, let's call it BestBioSolutions.

Alignment Case Study: Biotech Data Strategy

BestBioSolutions was focused on the research, development, and commercialization of biopesticides and bioherbicides. Biopesticides are pest control products that are derived from natural materials, including animals, plants, bacteria, and certain minerals.

Let's first look at the industry context in which BestBioSolutions operates.

What were the opportunities in this space? In other words, what was the potential upside for a biopesticide start-up?

First, the timing was right. There was a growing pressure— regulatory, environmental, and consumer-driven—to move away from synthetic chemicals in agriculture. Biopesticides, developed from naturally occurring materials such as microbes, plant extracts, or minerals, were increasingly seen as a viable path forward. They were often safer, more targeted, and better aligned with sustainable farming practices.

From a regulatory perspective, chemical pesticide approvals were becoming increasingly stringent. At the same time, many governments were actively encouraging biological alternatives, offering streamlined approval pathways or incentives to adopt cleaner technologies. This created a regulatory landscape that could work in favor of well-positioned biotech startups. Yet, there was also a regulatory challenge, as while some markets offered fast-tracks for biologics, others treated biopesticides almost like pharmaceuticals, requiring extensive toxicology studies, environmental impact assessments, and multi-year review cycles. Understanding where and how to launch could make or break early momentum.

From a consumer perspective, there was also an increasing demand. Major producers and retailers were pushing for cleaner, more transparent supply chains. If a startup could demonstrate that its product was effective, cost-competitive, and compliant with organic or sustainable certifications, there was real potential to be drawn in by grower demand.

Furthermore, technology itself was evolving. Advances in genomics, fermentation, and formulation science have enabled startups to develop more sophisticated products that are not only effective but also shelf-stable, scalable, and easier to apply in the field. That opened the door to product differentiation, IP defensibility, and long-term business value. Adding AI and ML capabilities to the mix allowed for a faster time to market and better cost competitiveness.

However, while opportunity was clear, this field was not without its challenges.

In addition to the regulatory hurdles that I had already mentioned, the biggest challenge in biopesticides was proving their effectiveness. Field efficacy had to be demonstrated across different geographies, crop types, and pest pressures. Unlike synthetic chemicals, which often work as broad-spectrum killers, biopesticides tend to be more selective and slower-acting.

Second, scaling production was non-trivial. The biopesticide that worked in a lab or greenhouse didn't always translate to large-scale production, packaging, and distribution. Startups needed to think early about process engineering, formulation stability, and logistics, while keeping unit costs competitive with legacy chemicals that have had decades to optimize their cost structures.

Lastly, the go-to-market strategy was complex. Most growers purchase through agronomic consultants, cooperatives, or crop input distributors, rather than directly from manufacturers. To break into those networks, a startup would have to build trust, showcase verifiable field trial results, and have a product that integrated neatly into existing application routines.

The BestBioSolutions vision was to make farming sustainable by providing eco-friendly pest control solutions that are as effective as chemical alternatives but far safer for the environment and human health.

To take advantage of the opportunities and to overcome the challenges inherent in the industry, all teams in BestBioSolutions were striving to accelerate the speed of creating, manufacturing, and getting approval for new biopesticides while maintaining quality and efficacy.

This business strategy can be summarized as "best in less": best compounds in less time and for less money.

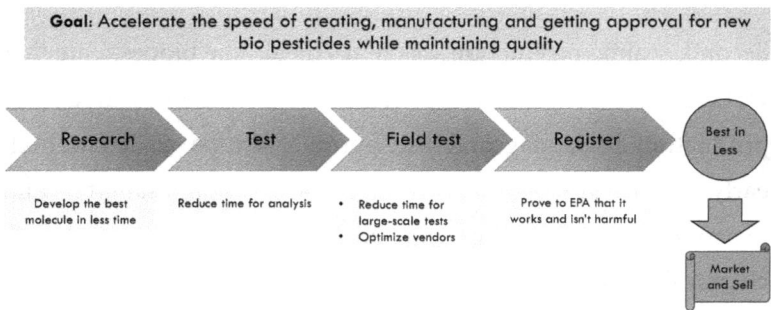

Goal: Accelerate the speed of creating, manufacturing and getting approval for new bio pesticides while maintaining quality

Research	Test	Field test	Register	Best in Less
Develop the best molecule in less time	Reduce time for analysis	• Reduce time for large-scale tests • Optimize vendors	Prove to EPA that it works and isn't harmful	

Market and Sell

Figure 11: Optimizing production pipeline for a biotech company.

BestBioSolutions had four major business teams: Research, Analysis, Operations, and Sales. It also had a Data and Analytics team that supported every business team. The question of my engagement was, "What is the most effective data strategy and roadmap to enable the 'Best in Less' strategy?"

Let's use the framework we've covered in the first part of the book to discover the value that data and analytics capabilities can bring to each of the business lines.

The first team was Research. This team was responsible for the discovery and screening, which involved searching for a biological agent that could suppress or eliminate agricultural pests. This often meant collecting hundreds—sometimes thousands—of samples from soil, plant surfaces, insect habitats, or marine environments. Each sample was tested to determine if it exhibited any pesticidal or antimicrobial activity. It was not enough to kill a pest once in a petri dish; the agent had to do so consistently and for the right reasons.

This was where modern biotech tools came in. Data and machine learning enabled high-throughput screening and genetic sequencing to help isolate promising candidates and understand their mechanisms of action. Most candidates didn't make it past this stage. They were either ineffective, unstable, or simply not scalable. But the few that passed offered the foundation for the next phase.

To meet the demands of the "best in less" strategy, the BestBioSolutions research team needed to accelerate and focus the discovery of the candidates and hone its process so that the researchers spent less time on unworkable candidates and moved through the screening tests faster and more effectively.

What data and data capabilities were important to achieve this goal?

First, data collection was crucial to have access to the inputs and outputs of all previous tests of potential agents, including those that failed and those that advanced to the next phase. That meant that BestBioSolutions researchers would have to move past the freestyle electronic notebooks and use tools that force much more structure on the data collected. This would be a big change management challenge for the BestBioSolutions' data team: the researchers were the stars of the company, and making a case that they would need to change how they went about their business was not for the faint of heart.

The second capability was Molecule MDM. In the absence of a unique identifier for each molecule assigned at the very beginning of the research process and carried through all the way to registering the successful compound, the overall process became very inefficient and labor-intensive. This would severely impede the achievement of the "best in less" goal.

Machine learning, analytics, and reporting rounded up the set of capabilities necessary for optimizing the research step. Machine learning was a differentiator for BestBioSolutions in producing the initial, highly focused set of candidates, while analytics and reporting provided full transparency into the process and opportunities for acceleration and improvement to both researchers and the leadership team.

The next team was the Analysis team. This team was responsible for narrowing down the list of candidates from research to those who could work beyond the lab. Researchers ran controlled tests to confirm that the candidate consistently performed against target pests, without harming crops, pollinators, or people.

This phase also assessed whether the candidate can be grown, harvested, or synthesized in a controlled environment. A product that could not be reliably reproduced was not commercially viable.

To achieve the "best for less" goal in this stage of the process, a detailed and structured collection of test data was no less important than in the first stage. It's also a change management challenge for the researchers conducting this analysis, but a slightly smaller one, as they would be the recipients of the benefits of having easy access to the data created in step 1. This would hold true for every subsequent stage—detailed and structured test data was key for all steps of this process. While a certain amount of resistance was to be expected from researchers and analysts conducting each step, the later stages of the process would have an easier time seeing the value, as they'd be the beneficiaries of the data collected up to their step in the process.

Molecule MDM continued to be fundamental in connecting the results of the research and analysis stages and informing both current and future development. The same held true for reporting and analytics: automated reporting would enable the analysis team to combine and analyze the results of all experiments simultaneously, significantly speeding up this stage of the process.

The next team was Operations. The operations team was responsible for two major steps: field testing and regulatory approval.

What are field tests? Once a product has a working prototype, it needs to prove itself under real conditions. Laboratory efficacy doesn't guarantee field performance, especially when dealing with variables such as weather, soil types, and pest behavior. Field trials are typically conducted across various regions, crops, and seasons to evaluate the performance of biopesticides over time.

These trials were essential for understanding how much of the product was needed, how often it must be applied, and what other conditions would affect its success. They also provided critical data for the next stage, which was regulatory approval. Additionally, they provided early feedback from growers, delivering data that informed commercial strategy and built credibility.

Field trials were also expensive and highly dependent on vendors who conducted them. The Best for Less goal for this stage was to reduce the time and cost of field tests.

The same three data capabilities —detailed and structured data collection, Molecule MDM, and reporting and analytics —were key for this stage for the same reasons. Additionally, to optimize the performance and cost of external vendors, connecting the results of the field tests to the vendors performing them, along with cost and timeliness information, a new data capability was needed: Vendor MDM.

The next step was regulatory approval. Regulatory bodies typically require evidence that the product is safe for humans, animals, and the environment, as well as proof that it works under defined conditions.

The submission process required detailed documentation of the product's composition, mechanism of action, field efficacy, and safety data. Getting it right the first time mattered a great deal, as regulatory delays can stall momentum and burn cash. After all, if a firm didn't have regulatory approval, it didn't have a product to sell, and thus, no revenue.

The regulatory approval step was the ultimate payoff of all the efforts and inconveniences of foregoing the free-form lab notes and collecting detailed data in a structured way, and having molecule MDM all the way from the first step. The ability to easily and quickly collate all testing and evidence in response to any question from the regulator would significantly accelerate the approval process, and this had a very direct impact on the "Best for Less" goal.

What comes after regulatory approval? Manufacturing at scale and selling! All the challenges of the sales and marketing process that we've discussed in an earlier chapter apply to BestBioSolutions. To address these challenges, Prospect/Client MDM (which has significant overlaps with Vendor MDM required for the field tests) and data governance of CRM and external data sources emerged as key considerations.

To recap, aligning data capabilities across all business teams of BestBioSolutions to achieve the goal of its business strategy, "Best for Less," established these priorities:

- **Molecule MDM was the backbone of the entire pipeline**: A unique, persistent identifier for each biological agent ensured traceability from discovery through regulatory approval. Without consistent molecule-level identity, it was impossible to link research, test results, and field performance, undermining both speed and quality of decision-making.

- **Detailed and structured data collection unlocked downstream acceleration**: From discovery to field trials, unstructured lab notes and fragmented documentation slowed down regulatory prep, repeat testing, and commercial validation. Enforcing structured data collection early created leverage later, accelerating speed, improving compliance, and decreasing cost.

- **Analytics and reporting drove operational clarity and strategic focus**: At every stage— R&D, proof of concept, field trials, and commercialization—teams needed the ability to analyze performance, spot patterns, and make resource allocation decisions. Transparent reporting also supported leadership oversight and external communication with regulators and investors.

- **Vendor MDM enabled scalable and cost-effective field testing**: Field trials depended heavily on external partners. Without a clear view into vendor performance, cost, and responsiveness across trials, BestBioSolutions couldn't optimize trial spend or timelines. Vendor MDM supported partner selection, evaluation, and accountability.

- **Prospect MDM was critical for commercial traction post-approval**: Once a product was ready to go to market, the same rigor used in R&D must apply to managing buyer data. Prospect MDM would support segmentation, outreach, and relationship management, particularly when navigating complex buyer ecosystems, such as those of agronomic consultants, co-ops, and growers.

Here is how the capability alignment map looked for the Best in Less strategy:

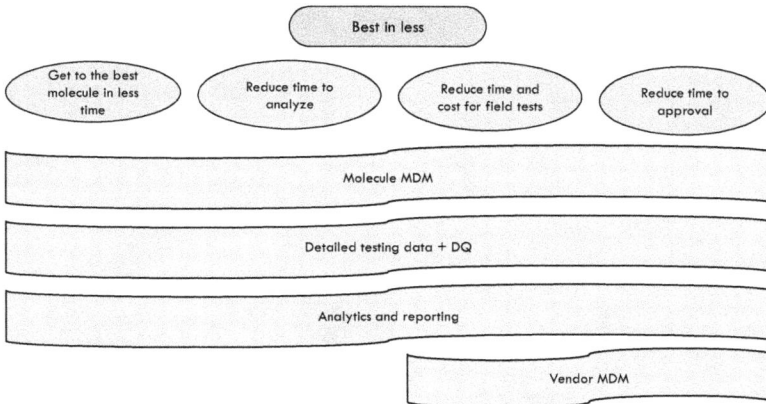

Figure 12: Optimizing biotech research–Data Capability strategy.

There are four strategic capabilities that BestBioSolutions could deploy to achieve its strategy, but building all four at the same time would have required more investment and more time than the company could afford. So, where should it have started?

That depended on its current level of data centricity. This strategic alignment step showed all the capabilities needed and tied them to specific business goals and strategies, thereby defining the target state. But to create a roadmap, the Data and Analytics team not only needed to know the destination but also to understand its starting point. What was its current level of data centricity?

CHAPTER FIVE

Evaluating Organizational Data Centricity

Now that we know which capabilities are needed to enable the business vision and strategy holistically across the enterprise, we need to understand the company's current position. After all, a roadmap is a set of directions on how to reach your target state. However, as with any directions, you need to know not only where you are going but also where you currently are.

Of course, there are many frameworks out there for evaluating the current state of capabilities. The one that I found most useful in my work with the clients is the Data Centricity Framework, first introduced by Peter Serenita in his CDO Magazine article, "The Data-Driven Organization." This framework provides a useful set of anchors to evaluate a company's current position and identify the best next steps, given its level of data centricity.

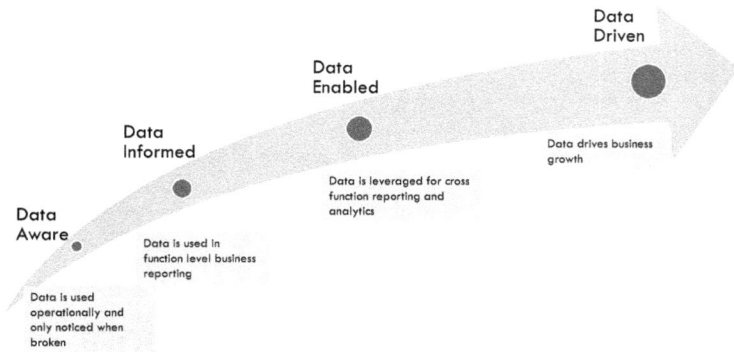

Data
Driven

Data
Enabled

Data
Informed

Data drives business
growth

Data
Aware

Data is leveraged for cross
function reporting and
analytics

Data is used in
function level business
reporting

Data is used
operationally and
only noticed when
broken

Figure 13: Evolution of data use.

This framework recognizes four stages of data centricity:

Stage 1: Data-Aware

At the Data-Aware stage of data centricity, organizations begin to recognize the presence and importance of data, but only within the confines of individual functions. Data is typically created as a byproduct of business processes, captured as a necessary outcome of executing a task. Each function owns and uses its own data independently, leading to siloed repositories that rarely communicate with one another. This isolation is reinforced by a "need-to-know" mindset, where data access is limited to what each team deems necessary for its specific operations. As a result, data is primarily used for short-term, transactional needs rather than for cross-functional insight or long-term decision-making. The organization may have a growing awareness of data's value, but it lacks the integration, accessibility, and strategic alignment needed to extract its full potential.

It's worth noting that Data-Aware companies generate and utilize a significant amount of data. However, they often lack the necessary data capabilities to leverage it effectively for business purposes. The capabilities they do have are very manual, such as screen scraping or Excel plug-ins. It's also worth noting that even in the companies at a higher data maturity level, there are sometimes pockets of Data-Aware functions tucked away. For example, some Wall Street equity analysis and research work is heavily reliant on Excel plugins to bring data into enormous spreadsheets (that often can't handle the volume and complexity) and then slice and dice using Excel macros, finally exporting into PowerPoint without ever touching a production data repository. This situation persists, not because there aren't any better and more efficient ways to bring this data in, analyze it, and publish it to subscribers, but because of the cultural "we've always done it that way" mindset and distrust of enterprise technology or data teams.

So, if a company is in a Data-Aware stage, what value can it extract from its data and its highly manual data capabilities? While limited, there is still some tactical value in using data both for offense and defense, even if process inefficiencies and tool limitations constrain that value.

On the offense side, data is often used for manual business reporting and analytics. Analysts build point-in-time dashboards or spreadsheets to track sales, volume, or product performance within a single function. There may also be some **use of external data sources**, such as industry benchmarks, customer lists, or market intelligence providers, to generate insights. However, this is typically done outside of core business processes and is rarely integrated into broader decision-making.

On the defense side, some teams utilize data for manual business risk evaluation, such as basic financial risk scoring or compliance reviews. However, the absence of integrated systems means that these evaluations often rely on individuals manually pulling and validating data across disparate sources. Opportunities to monetize data or utilize it to drive operational efficiency are limited because assembling the data to understand a process end-to-end is already a significant effort.

What can AI do at this point?

In a Data-Aware organization, AI is not yet a core part of the operating model. However, it can still be utilized in focused, practical ways that add value without requiring a perfect data foundation. One of the most immediate opportunities is to use AI-enabled tools to accelerate data management capability development, such as, for example, automating metadata tagging, identifying data quality issues, or suggesting relationships between disconnected datasets. AI can also help make internal unstructured data more usable, such as extracting key information from documents, emails, or call transcripts that would otherwise remain inaccessible.

There is also value in applying AI to external data, for instance, to summarize trends from public sources or benchmark performance against competitors. Additionally, AI can be deployed in targeted business functions, such as call centers, chatbots, or marketing content generation, where models can enhance responsiveness, reduce manual work, and support customer engagement, even in the absence of tightly integrated internal data.

While AI in a Data-Aware company cannot drive strategic transformation, it can deliver real, incremental improvements. These early wins also help build momentum for broader data initiatives by demonstrating how intelligent automation can support both business and technology teams.

Stage 2: Data-Informed

At the Data-Informed stage, organizations begin to move beyond the basic operational use of data and start leveraging it to support decision-making, albeit in a limited and fragmented manner. Data is still primarily created as a byproduct of business processes and remains siloed within individual functions. However, selective sharing starts to occur, typically through custom-built pipelines into business line data warehouses, where data is transformed and made available for specific use cases. These integrations are often ad hoc, built to meet specific reporting needs rather than as part of a cohesive enterprise strategy. Access to data continues to follow a "need-to-know" philosophy, with visibility restricted based on functional roles or reporting lines. Despite these constraints, data begins to play a role in shaping decisions, marking a shift from purely transactional use toward more analytical applications. Still, without consistent standards or enterprise-wide coordination, the value extracted remains limited and uneven.

What can organizations actually do with data at this stage?

On the offense side, most business lines can generate automated insights within their own domains. For example, a sales team may be able to track performance by region and channel through its own dashboards, and the finance team may have a working view of expense trends. However, these views are narrow. Cross-business reporting and analytics still rely on manual work, requiring analysts to pull data from different sources, clean it, and build one-off dashboards that are hard to maintain or reuse.

On the defense side, companies can implement automated risk evaluation within individual functions, such as loan risk scoring or transaction monitoring. These processes are typically well-integrated into the business line systems and generate operational value.

What cannot be done at this stage reflects the limitations of siloed thinking. There's no enterprise-level efficiency driven by shared data. Furthermore, there's also no enterprise-wide capability for regulatory, financial, or risk reporting, which means that large-scale compliance or audit efforts still involve scrambling for disconnected data and manually reconciling inconsistencies. On the commercial ("offense") side, cross-functional reporting and analytics can't be automated, and there is still no single view of the customer, making coordinated outreach or customer lifetime value management impossible.

What can AI do at this point? In a Data-Informed organization, AI has more room to create value, but it still depends heavily on the quality and consistency of the underlying data. AI tools can be used to generate business line insights by combining internal, external, and unstructured data sources, even if the systems are not fully integrated. This is where generative AI and natural language models can help surface patterns or trends that would otherwise be buried in documents, call transcripts, or survey responses.

Similar to the Data-Aware stage, AI can be used to accelerate data management capabilities, such as automating metadata tagging, suggesting data mappings, or identifying anomalies across datasets. These tools help the data team move faster without waiting for full architectural redesigns. Additionally, AI can support tactical needs in call centers, chatbots, and marketing content generation, creating short-term wins even as foundational data capabilities continue to mature.

At this stage, AI cannot reliably deliver high-impact enterprise AI solutions, such as advanced personalization, real-time optimization, or intelligent decision-making, across departments. These use cases require more consistent, accessible, and governed data than most Data-Informed organizations have. But that doesn't mean AI should wait; if used wisely, it can drive visible value, help build internal momentum, and prepare the organization for what comes next.

Stage 3: Data-Enabled

At the Data-Enabled stage, organizations take a significant step toward achieving enterprise-wide data integration and decision support. While data is still created as a byproduct of business processes, it is no longer confined to individual silos. Instead, it is systematically consolidated into enterprise data warehouses and lakes, where it is transformed, organized, and made accessible across functions. In addition to cross-functional reporting, this infrastructure supports decision intelligence, where data is actively used to drive operational and strategic choices. Access shifts from a "need-to-know" to a "need-to-use" model, expanding availability while maintaining appropriate controls. Internal operational data is now integrated with external sources, providing decision-makers with a more comprehensive and timely view of their business environment. Data governance has matured beyond policy into an active oversight function, ensuring quality, consistency, and accountability across domains. Data management capabilities are increasingly applied at the point of consumption, supporting the development of scalable and reusable data products. As a result, reliance on ad hoc tools like Excel diminishes, replaced by governed, enterprise-grade platforms that support advanced analytics and automation. This stage marks a turning point: data becomes a reliable enabler of business performance, not just a reference point.

What can companies at the Data-Enabled stage achieve with their data?

On the efficiency front, they can now significantly reduce the time and cost it takes to deliver outcomes across functions. This includes improvements in areas like marketing, sales forecasting, customer service, user experience, corporate finance, and compliance. These gains come from having a shared view of business activity and the ability to act on it quickly.

On the offense side, automated, enterprise-level reporting and analytics are now possible. Companies can track end-to-end performance, link operational drivers to financial outcomes, and optimize decisions with greater confidence. On the defense side, the organization can now rely on accurate and trusted reporting for compliance, audit, and risk management, supported by consistent data lineage and validation.

However, there is a structural limitation. Even though enterprise data environments exist, the systems and processes that feed them are still siloed and inconsistent. This means the efforts required to make data usable, such as cleaning, mapping, and reconciling, are substantial and ongoing. In many cases, the cost of maintaining these environments can exceed the efficiency gains they're supposed to deliver. For companies in this position, it often makes the most sense to anchor their data strategy in a few high-value domains, such as top-line growth or risk mitigation, where the returns are measurable and immediate.

What can AI do at this point?

At the Data-Enabled stage, organizations are in a strong position to begin using AI more broadly. Because core data is now integrated and governed, AI tools can be used to produce enterprise-level business insights by pulling together structured, unstructured, and external data to identify patterns, forecast outcomes, or generate recommendations. This opens the door to a more strategic use of AI in areas such as customer segmentation, pricing optimization, and forecasting.

As in previous stages, AI can still be used to accelerate internal data management workflows and support tactical use cases, such as marketing content creation, customer support chatbots, and call center summarization, where it can handle repetitive tasks and enhance responsiveness.

Still, most AI efforts at this stage are focused on augmentation rather than full automation. AI tools help people move faster and see further, but they still rely on a strong human in the loop to interpret context, validate outputs, and take action. For AI to play a larger operational role, the company will need to tackle the deeper architectural and cultural shifts associated with the next stage: Data-Driven.

Stage 4: Data-Driven

At the Data-Driven stage, the organization undergoes a fundamental shift: data is no longer a byproduct of business processes; it *is* the product. Business functions are structured around data assets, treating them as core components of value creation rather than support tools. Data is no longer replicated or segregated by function. Instead, there is a single source of truth that is accessed by all, with the operational model moving functions to the data rather than duplicating the data for each function. An "always share" philosophy governs access—data is open by default, with restrictions applied only where necessary. This cultural shift enables data to not only inform or enable decisions, but to actively drive behavior, products, and innovation.

Systems architecture is designed from the ground up to support Data-Driven operations, with seamless interoperability and scalability. Governance is no longer a separate discipline; it is embedded in everyday business activity, supported by clearly defined roles, automated controls, and continuous stewardship. Tools like Excel become largely obsolete, replaced by integrated platforms that provide real-time access, analysis, and automation on a large scale. At this stage, data is not just an asset; it is the foundation upon which the organization operates, competes, and grows.

It's a huge challenge for a company that hasn't started in a Data-Driven way to become one.

If a company is already Data-Enabled, the first capability to shift into the Data-Driven stage must be cultural—that is, clear and ever-present prioritization of data-driven product, process, and technology decisions. A Data-Enabled to Data-Driven transition is huge from the technology and architecture perspective, and it entails not only new ways of working but also a highly risky re-platforming of essential business applications. Not many companies with legacy technology footprints can take either the expense or the risk of such fundamental change. Yet, if they do—for example, by moving to the cloud or deciding to rearchitect their business operational systems because the old ones no longer work —putting data at the center of this transformation is key to achieving the outsize returns from this type of investment. However, I have rarely seen companies do that, and the reason for this is cultural—business and technology leaders do not understand the enormous upside of taking the data-driven approach.

So, what becomes possible at the Data-Driven stage?

On the efficiency front, all business processes can now be made straight-through and automated, with no manual reconciliation required. There is no longer a need to check and recheck data across systems—every team, product, and process runs on the same real-time foundation. Internal handoffs disappear, decision delays are reduced, and the cost of process management drops significantly.

On the offense side, the potential is no longer constrained by data access or integration bottlenecks. At this stage, the organization's ability to utilize data is limited only by imagination, budget, and constraints such as compliance, privacy, and ethical considerations. Data can be used to create entirely new products and services, power predictive capabilities at scale, and drive hyper-personalized customer experiences—all in production, not just as prototypes.

What can AI do at this point?

In a Data-Driven company, AI reaches its full potential. It is no longer confined to isolated use cases or pilot projects. With unified, real-time, and high-quality data available across the business, AI can be embedded directly into core operations. This includes automated decision-making, autonomous workflows, predictive forecasting, real-time personalization, and truly differentiating customer experience.

AI also helps organizations manage themselves more efficiently. It powers data management automation, surfaces metadata relationships, flags anomalies, recommends governance actions, and helps keep the data ecosystem aligned with business goals without requiring constant human oversight.

Still, there are limits to AI and data use, except that they are not technical. AI and data use must still respect regulatory, privacy, security, and ethical constraints. This includes data sharing and usage that may be technically possible but crosses legal or societal boundaries. For example, using behavioral data in ways that breach consumer trust or manipulating decision outcomes through opaque algorithms still violates both governance standards and organizational principles, no matter how advanced the systems are. The technology may be capable of almost anything, but the organization still needs to decide what it should do, not just what it can.

One very important point about this data centricity framework is that it is not a maturity framework, meaning companies do not need to go through the first three stages to reach the Data-Driven stage. In fact, if a company is in the Data-Aware stage, it'll be best served to create a roadmap that will transition it into the Data-Driven stage, completely bypassing both the Data-Informed and Data-Enabled stages. And if a company is a startup, it should start as a Data-Driven company and avoid the downsides of disconnected, siloed data of uncertain quality. That's one of the huge advantages of a startup—it's a lot easier and cheaper to become Data-Driven from the get-go than try to transition there after accumulating all the bad habits of Data-Informed and Data-Enabled stages.

For organizations in the Data-Aware stage, the next best set of actions is to focus on creating company-wide alignment and laying the groundwork for consistent data use across teams. The first critical action is to launch an executive-led, company-wide Data Literacy Program. This step creates a shared language and builds awareness across all levels of the organization about how data can and should be used, taking it beyond a technical concept into a business growth driver. Without this foundational understanding, even the most effective tools and systems will struggle to gain traction.

In parallel, companies need to modernize their technology stack to make internal data more accessible and usable across functions. This includes breaking down silos, enabling more real-time access to operational data, and reducing the reliance on spreadsheets and point solutions. Finally, organizations should develop core data management capabilities, both on the business and technology sides. This involves establishing the necessary roles, processes, and systems to manage data as a business asset, encompassing metadata, data quality, data ownership, and access controls.

If organizations in the Data-Aware stage take care to develop and implement a value-driven data strategy, they can avoid the trial-and-error cycle that often occurs in the Data-Informed and Data-Enabled stages. By setting the right foundation early, before too many bad habits take root, they have the opportunity to **leapfrog their competitors** and move directly into a more Data-Driven operating model. That model is faster, more efficient, and better aligned with long-term business goals.

To make these concepts more real, let's go back to the Customer Lifetime Value (CLV) and see how the ability to calculate this very important metric depends on the data centricity of a company. We will adapt our usual business case study approach and perform a thought exercise using an example of a fictional bank—let's call it BestBank, and a fictional customer—let's call him John Smith, to illustrate how the ability to calculate and leverage CLV changes at different levels of BestBank's data centricity.

Let's go back in time, about 20 years ago, when BestBank was in its Data-Aware stage. It offered services to retail and small business customers. Its retail services included checking and savings accounts, credit cards, and mortgages. Its services for small business customers included business entity checking and savings accounts. BestBank was organized into two business lines, each operating on a separate technology platform. Moreover, each of the product lines in the consumer bank business also operated separately, including separate sales, customer services, and technology teams and platforms.

John Smith became a customer of BestBank when he received a credit card from them upon starting college. He was duly onboarded into the credit card system, and that was the only place where his information was stored. Then, after he graduated and started working, he opened a checking account in BestBank to deposit his paychecks. Since BestBank was at the Data-Aware stage, checking account teams and systems had no visibility into information in the credit card business, and so he was onboarded as a new BestBank customer into the checking account platform, with a different ID and with a slight variation on his name. The same thing happened a few years later when John Smith obtained a mortgage from BestBank: he again was treated by the mortgage team as new to the bank customer (even though his application showed his checking account with BestBank) and assigned yet another id under yet another variation of his name: in this system he was John D. Smith. Could BestBank at that point determine an accurate CLV for John? No, it couldn't, since there was no way for

BestBank to connect John Smith of the credit card to J. Smith of the checking account to John D. Smith of the mortgage. Because of BestBank's inability to see all of John's accounts, it didn't offer any differentiated or personalized experience to John. In effect, John's loyalty went unrewarded.

A few years passed, and BestBank had moved forward in its data journey and created a retail business data warehouse, bringing together the data from its credit card, checking accounts, and mortgage systems, and connecting all the different representations of John's relationship with the bank. And BestBank now looked at John's CLV[4], recognized his loyalty, and kicked its service and outreach to John up a notch.

But then John decided to open his own business: JS LLC. As always, he went to BestBank to open a checking account for JS LLC, expecting the banker to recognize him as a long-standing customer and offer an upgraded account and service. Alas, this was not to be. While BestBank invested in bringing together data from its retail business line, it hasn't yet started on its enterprise data enablement journey, and so its corporate business customer service and operations teams had no way of knowing who John was. Nevertheless, John stayed loyal and became a customer of BestBank corporate business.

---

[4] As discussed in Chapter 3 CLV business case study, BestBank would not only need to combine and connect customer information but product information as well.

With mounting regulatory pressures and increased competition, BestBank embarked on an enterprise-wide data strategy. As part of this strategy, it created an enterprise data lake, combining data from its multiple business lines. Now, finally, all of John's activities across all of his accounts came together in one place and became visible not only to him through the BestBank website and app but also to any customer service representative, be it in the branches or on the phone. As a result, BestBank could finally see the full picture of John's involvement with the bank, appreciate his loyalty, and treat him as the valuable customer he's been all along. From John's perspective, his customer experience improved significantly at every touchpoint he had with the bank, and his loyalty was finally appreciated.

From the BestBank perspective, however, calculating CLV for customers with multiple relationships with the bank, while possible and key for the increase of the top line, remained expensive and ate into its bottom line, and negated some of the benefits it realized with moving into the data-enabled level of data centricity.

Finally, ongoing competitive pressure, ever-increasing cost of BestBank's legacy technology stack, and the desire to take advantage of rapidly developing cloud and AI capabilities to further grow the business, led BestBank to embark on a risky, yet highly rewarding cloud transformation initiative that aimed to modernize its front office technology stack and move it to the cloud. BestBank approached this initiative from a data-first perspective, not only updating its technology infrastructure but also doing the hard work of reviewing, modernizing, and standardizing its business processes, starting all the way from marketing and sales, through to customer onboarding, to credit risk assessment, KYC compliance, and financial reporting. As a result of this multi-year effort, BestBank became a truly data-driven company, reaping enormous benefits in end-to-end efficiencies, straight-through processing, a data-driven customer experience, and the ability to leverage its data, analytics, and AI innovations for any business strategy. Coincidentally, the calculation of the CLV metric for its customers became easy and stopped eating into its bottom line, allowing BestBank to derive all the benefits of knowing CLV for all of its customers.

How did John notice this transformation? As an already valued customer, John began to notice that actions that used to take effect overnight or sometimes longer, such as processing deposits or opening a new account on the app, now happened almost instantly. He also noticed an increased rate of innovative products and services coming from BestBank, making him glad that he had remained its customer for all these years.

While this story amalgamates the experiences of many individuals with various banks, it illustrates how both the customer experience and internal efficiency of the bank change across different states of data centricity. It also shows that a company's business data strategy heavily depends not only on its near-term and long-term goals, but also on its current state of data capabilities and its associated gaps.

- **Data centricity is not a linear path**: Progression through the stages unlocks major business value, but each stage brings its own challenges and investment requirements.

- **Technology alone is not enough**: Success depends on cultural readiness, leadership alignment, and clarity of strategic priorities. Without cultural transformation, technology transformation will overpromise and underdeliver.

- **The biggest leap is from Data-Enabled to Data-Driven**: This transition demands not just new architecture, but a new way of thinking: decisions, value, and organizational structure must all shift.

- **The earlier the commitment, the greater the return**: Embedding Data-Driven thinking early accelerates value realization and reduces rework later on.

CHAPTER SIX

Creating a
Data Capability Roadmap

How does the Data Centricity Framework inform the creation of a data capability roadmap? Evaluating the current state of the company through data-centricity lenses creates a clear starting point and informs what capabilities of the target state ought to be built first.

We now have two powerful frameworks to create a value-driven roadmap: the Business Value Framework and the Data Centricity Framework.

The Business Value Framework serves two primary goals: it aligns data capabilities with the business vision and strategy, and it informs the target state of data capabilities to enable the achievement of its mission and business goals. It also clearly shows the tradeoffs in risk and value between different options and capabilities.

The Data Centricity Framework allows companies to understand where they are currently, what the next best steps are, and also what challenges they are facing and, frankly, whether the data-driven stage is even achievable, since for some companies the data-enabled state is the best they can strive for given their current state and legacy technology and operations footprint.

Let's demonstrate how the data-centricity framework informs the creation of the roadmap by revisiting the BestBioSolutions business case.

Figure 14 shows where we left BestBioSolutions on its journey to create a growth-driven data strategy.

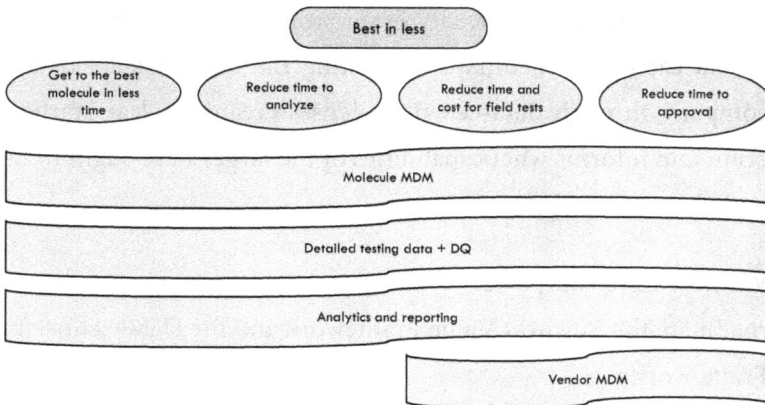

Figure 14: Reaching "No-Kill 2025–Data Capability strategy.

The question now is which one of these capabilities was the best first step for BestBioSolutions? What would bring the most value in the least amount of time while serving as a foundation for the next set of capabilities?

Let's use the Data Centricity Framework and assess where BestBioSolutions was in terms of its data centricity.

Like many companies in the real world, BestBioSolutions was in between two levels: Data-Aware and Data-Enabled.

On one hand, it implemented Molecule MDM throughout its processes, from the very first step of research all the way through operations and regulatory approval. This was an enormous advantage over many incumbents in this industry who still struggled with unifying the most important outcomes of their business: the compounds they produce across multiple business lines.

Its analytics and data science functions were excellent as well, relying on modern cloud-based data technologies and being highly leveraged by business teams across the entire production pipeline.

On the other hand, the foundation of value and differentiation in the company, the Research team, used electronic notebooks to record and manage their process, as is standard in most startups in the biotech space, resulting in highly unstructured and difficult to leverage data, impeding the work of the analysis and operations teams that were heavily relying on this data.

Additionally, vendor management, which was one of the major levers of achieving "best in less" in the operations team, was highly manual, relying heavily on spreadsheets, emails, and documents. While this structure was justified at the scale at which

BestBioSolutions was operating, a more automated vendor management system would have positioned them better for future growth.

The Sales and Marketing function had a similar issue with their CRM system being run off of spreadsheets, which is not the ideal state for achieving "best in less".

While these choices were made at the time that BestBioSolutions was a small startup, the company ran the risk of outgrowing these solutions and not being ideally positioned to derive value from data in its aspirational future state.

Given this current state, Figure 15 shows how BestBioSolutions assessed each of the capabilities on value versus cost and the complexity scale.

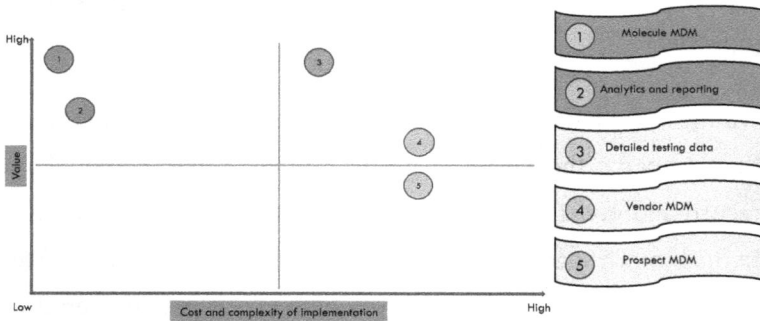

Figure 15: Value versus cost and complexity.

Transforming the research and analysis process to create detailed, structured, and standardized data, while not easy to implement, was of the highest value to BestBioSolutions, given its current stage of data centricity and the first step in BestBioSolutions' data strategy. A big part of this step was managing change and resistance from the research and analysis teams, for whom the switch from electronic notebooks to more structured software was non-trivial. This is where the power of the business value framework shone: the process of discovering and aligning value to the company's mission and communicating it clearly throughout, created both top management support and enough understanding among the researchers to comply with the change, some occasional grumbling aside. It also helped with funding since in startups funding can be a zero-sum game: allocating money to the data projects reduced the amount of funding available to the other teams, so only by building this understanding of how key this effort was for the success of everyone in the company could this funding be allocated and not taken back when times got hard.

What about the field test Vendor MDM? There was a direct line between having a full picture of field test vendors and the efficiency and effectiveness of the field test process. Moreover, Vendor MDM had a large overlap with prospect MDM, which was necessary to accelerate the sales and marketing funnel as we've discussed previously. And later, prospect MDM could be easily scaled to become customer MDM and driving CLV, retention, and cross-sell. However, accelerating sales and marketing and retaining customers were not yet the problems BestBioSolutions was facing at this stage; it first needed to get the product approved. That meant it needed to make its bio pesticide discovery, testing, and approval processes as effective and as efficient as possible.

To summarize, as a result of going through this process, BestBioSolutions transformed a list of data projects into a strategic, value-aligned roadmap.

Step 1: Structure Research and Analysis Data

This data was stored in a mix of electronic notebooks, free-form spreadsheets, and custom tools used by each team. Everyone worked in the way that felt most comfortable, but that comfort came at a cost. When it was time to determine what worked and why, or to compile the documentation for regulatory approval, the team often had to piece things together manually, often under tight timelines.

This step was about creating and enforcing structure by rolling out tools that captured standardized data, enforced basic data integrity, and linked back to the Molecule MDM. It also meant changing habits, especially in the research team, which was used to more open-ended workflows.

This step unlocked speed, quality, and transparency. It shortened the time from discovery to analysis, avoided duplication of effort, and made the entire process more resilient. It also reduced risk when things needed to be reconstructed to answer questions from the regulators. While change management here was tough, the payoff was huge, especially in the downstream stages that relied on reliable inputs from research and analysis.

Step 2: Bring Analytics into Focus

This step was about connecting existing reports and dashboards to the newly structured data and building a shared layer where people can see what was working, where things were stuck, and what needed attention. Whether that was tracking how long it took a candidate to move from discovery to field trial or seeing which trial vendors were consistently late or over budget, this layer created accuracy and insight.

Reporting and analytics served as the connective tissue, bringing visibility and insight across the organization. They allowed leadership to prioritize resources, enabled teams to identify process bottlenecks, and gave everyone a better understanding of what's working.

Step 3: Enable Field Testing Efficiency

Implement Vendor MDM to improve field testing cost, speed, and accountability. Field trials were expensive, and BestBioSolutions conducted a large number of them. However, there was no centralized way to track which vendors were performing what tasks, how effectively they were doing so, or whether they were worth the cost. That's where Vendor MDM came in.

This capability involved consolidating all scattered vendor information, including performance, cost, timelines, and trial results, into a single location and linking it to the rest of the process. Once that happened, it would be much easier to make decisions: Which vendors should we use again? Where are we losing time? What's the true cost per compound of getting through field trials?

Vendor MDM created operational efficiency. It made field testing faster, cheaper, and more reliable. And because field trial results fed into regulatory filings and go-to-market decisions, the benefits went beyond just cost control.

Step 4: Prepare for Growth

The last step in the roadmap prepared BestBioSolutions for what comes after regulatory approval—selling. Sales in this industry are complex, encompassing multiple distribution partners. To do this effectively, BestBioSolutions needed to identify those key players, understand their influence on each other, and develop and maintain the relationships.

Prospect MDM was about mapping and organizing the buyer ecosystem. It meant integrating CRM data, cleaning up external sources, and making sure the company wasn't operating off disconnected spreadsheets once commercial operations significantly expanded.

While this wasn't immediately urgent, it would become critical the moment regulatory approval was secured. Without it, sales and marketing would start at a disadvantage. With it, the company could hit the ground running with targeted outreach, clearer segmentation, and a tighter feedback loop between the field and the business.

Each step in this roadmap is built on the last, both technically and organizationally. It was a deliberately sequenced path designed to unlock real business value at every stage of BestBioSolutions' growth—from early R&D to scaled commercialization.

The Broader Lesson: Build with the End in Mind

By anchoring its roadmap in both business value and data-centricity frameworks, BestBioSolutions avoided the all-too-common mistake of building capabilities in a vacuum. Instead, it focused on what matters: speed, cost-efficiency, and scalability, delivered through smart, sequenced data investments.

In doing so, it built the capabilities —organizational, operational, and technical —that would enable it to scale with confidence and agility in the years to come.

Now let's step away from the real world BestBioSolutions, and use the particulars of this case study for a thought exercise that would illustrate how the level of data centricity in the company would influence the roadmap.

How would the roadmap have been different had BestBioSolutions been at a different stage of data centricity?

First, if BestBioSolutions were at the Data-Aware stage, what would it mean to the roadmap? Let's consider how

BestBioSolutions' technical and operational landscape would look at the Data-Aware stage.

The main features of the Data-Aware stage are:

- Data is seen as a byproduct of business processes.
- Processes and data are disparate and disconnected.

How would that manifest in BestBioSolutions?

The research team would be reliant on electronic lab notebooks to support its research activities. There would be no common registry of any new molecules and compounds being created and tested by the research team. When the likely candidates were identified and moved on to the next stage of the process, the analysis team would use its own software to keep track of its work, making traceability to the research data highly manual. The same would continue with field testing: the operations team would also use its own software. Each team would have its own reporting, mostly manual and Excel-based. However, there would be no way to connect the same molecules across different phases of the process, and there would also be no way to inform research on new compounds using the results of analysis and field testing.

As a result, collecting information necessary for regulatory approval would be a complex and highly manual undertaking.

On the plus side, every team would be very comfortable with the software and the processes it uses for its work, requiring limited training and support from the IT teams.

At this stage, the highest value data effort would be the creation of Molecule MDM and using the common unique identifier to connect all the research and analysis created by the different teams. Simply doing this would create significant value for the company and accelerate its journey towards the "Best for Less" goal.

Here is how the overall roadmap would look:

Step 1: Start with Molecule MDM

The first and most critical capability in this case is Molecule Master Data Management (MDM). This involves creating a unique, persistent identifier for each biological agent in the pipeline, from early research through analysis, field testing, and ultimately, regulatory submission.

Molecule MDM is foundational. It creates a single source of truth that connects every part of the pipeline. It enables the acceleration of discovery, avoidance of rework, and rapid response to regulatory questions. Without it, nothing downstream can scale cleanly or efficiently. This is the first capability that BestBioSolutions needs to move into the Data-Driven stage.

Step 2 and Step 3: Structure Research Data and Build Reporting & Analytics—Together

The subsequent phase of the roadmap is not a straightforward transition from one project to the next; rather, it is an iterative process. The implementation of Molecule MDM introduces the capacity to link and trace data across the full research pipeline, naturally prompting the question, "What insights can be derived from this newly connected information?" At this point, reporting and analytics take on a central role. The benefits are tangible and quickly produced. For example, the dashboards that monitor candidate progression, aggregate test results, and visualize trial timelines would be immediately valuable.

However, this phase introduces a new set of challenges. The availability of initial insights often leads to a surge in demand. As leadership becomes aware of the new analytical capabilities, expectations grow; teams seek increasingly granular views of the data, and the reporting function can become overwhelmed with requests. Without careful planning, efforts risk becoming reactive, with resources consumed by the production of one-off reports rather than the development of a scalable reporting foundation.

To address this, it is essential to advance structured data capture in parallel with reporting development. While unstructured lab notes and ad hoc spreadsheets may suffice for early insights, they are insufficient for long-term analytics needs. Reports built on inconsistent or poorly defined data structures will ultimately need to be reconstructed. A more sustainable approach involves two concurrent workstreams: initiating reporting where data quality is already sufficient, while simultaneously introducing structured data practices that will support more robust and scalable reporting in future iterations.

At this stage of the roadmap execution, BestBioSolutions would start to shift from a reactive to a proactive approach. Reporting would create visibility, help identify bottlenecks, and provide leadership with the information they need to guide the business. Structured research data, in turn, would ensure those insights are based on reliable, reusable inputs. The two capabilities would reinforce each other, and together they would create the foundation for the company to scale insight alongside operations.

The remaining steps are the same as before.

Step 4: Vendor MDM

Step 5: Prospect MDM into Client MDM

It's important to note that executing on this roadmap would move BestBioSolutions to the Data-Driven stage, bypassing all the bad habits that come with the highly siloed data-informed stage that a lot of their competitors are still trying to overcome.

Continuing our thought exercise, how would this roadmap be different if BestBioSolutions were in the Data-Informed stage?

Here are the characteristics of the Data-Informed stage:

- Data is still seen as a byproduct of a process.
- Each business line has its own data environment to enable line-of-business reporting.

The Data-Informed stage, while providing some data-related benefits to each of the business teams via siloed reporting, is actually harder to manage than the Data-Aware stage. Why is that? There is still no company-wide Molecule MDM; yet, each business line has its own way of identifying molecules—and they are all different. Connecting them together is a hard and expensive proposition, much more so than in the Data-Aware stage when there are no bad habits to break and no internal systems to re-engineer. In this case, Molecule MDM, while still foundational, is no longer the best candidate for the first step in the value driven roadmap—it's too big of a change both technically and culturally to create value fast: remember that a major characteristic of a value driven roadmap is frequent and early delivery of incremental value to the business.

Here are the steps of the data roadmap in the data-informed stage:

Step 1: Build End-to-End Reporting and Analytics Capability

The first step in the roadmap is to create a shared view across the pipeline. In a Data-Informed company, business teams utilize data frequently. However, each team uses its own systems, definitions, and reporting tools, and none of them connect. The research team tracks candidate progress using its own setup, the analysis team logs results in a different format, and operations rely on spreadsheets to monitor field trials. These environments function well enough locally, but they don't work together.

What BestBioSolutions needs most at this stage is a way to bring these fragmented views together into a coherent whole. Building end-to-end reporting would rely on leveraging existing systems to create a central layer of visibility, providing leadership with insights into how candidates move across teams, where timelines are lagging, and where the company is spending time and money without a clear return.

This first step involves creating visibility and exposing hidden inefficiencies in the process. Even if the data isn't clean yet, bringing it together in one place reveals where the gaps are and what needs fixing. It builds the case for deeper investment in data structure and governance, using evidence from real operational pain points.

Step 2: Roll Out Structured Testing Data and Molecule MDM Together, by Business Line

The main challenge in the Data-Informed stage is that its data is inconsistent and hard to connect. Each business line has already developed its own method for capturing and labeling molecules, and each uses different formats and tools to record test results. These habits are deeply embedded in the way people work. Trying to force a company-wide Molecule MDM into that environment without addressing how data is captured on a day-to-day basis is likely to fail.

The smarter path forward is to improve structure and consistency in each business line simultaneously as Molecule MDM is introduced. These two efforts need to move together, in a cross-iterative rollout that starts where the payoff is biggest and then expands. This approach keeps the work grounded in real use cases and avoids overwhelming any one team.

In Research

The research team needs to adopt structured tools for logging candidate molecules, their associated test designs, and results. Every new biological agent should be assigned a unique identifier that remains associated with it throughout the remainder of the process. Standardizing this upfront allows early screening results to be traced and reused later. Alongside this, basic dashboards can start to show research progress, capturing how many candidates are active, how many drop off, and where screening is taking too long.

In Analysis

Structured data from research must carry into analysis. Test outcomes must be logged using standardized formats and linked directly to the molecule IDs introduced upstream. This allows results to be compared across experiments and over time. Reporting here helps the team track which types of compounds perform best and which testing protocols yield the most consistent results.

In Field Testing

By the time compounds reach field trials, their molecule IDs should already be in place. Field test data—application conditions, environmental factors, trial outcomes—should be captured in a structured format and linked to both the compound and the vendor executing the trial. Reporting at this stage connects compound performance to operational execution, helping the company learn faster from each round of testing.

Pairing structured data collection with Molecule MDM keeps the work relevant to each team's goals while gradually building company-wide consistency. It would allow this version of BestBioSolutions to reduce rework, improve transparency, and accelerate decision-making without trying to fix everything at once. The result is a more connected pipeline with better data at every stage.

As before, Steps 4 and 5 stay the same: Vendor MDM and Prospect MDM.

To summarize, the roadmap for BestBioSolutions were it a Data-Informed company would focus on building upon existing solutions and evolving them to work better together.

By starting with reporting, then layering in structured data and Molecule MDM in a targeted way, BestBioSolutions can gradually shift from reactive data use to connected, insight-driven operations. Vendor and prospect MDM would then build on that foundation, helping the company move from development to commercialization without losing momentum along the way.

To summarize, we have conducted a deep dive into BestBioSolutions' business case study to illustrate how to leverage the Business Value of Data and Data Centricity frameworks to create a strategic, business value-aligned roadmap. This case study shows how a focused, structured approach to data strategy can unlock meaningful business results. Faced with a complex product development lifecycle and a demanding regulatory environment, the company resisted the common urge to chase quick wins or implement disconnected tools. Instead, it built a data roadmap anchored in business priorities and sequenced according to its real-world operating conditions.

By aligning data capabilities with clearly defined goals such as speed, cost efficiency, and scalability, BestBioSolutions moved beyond project lists and laid the foundation for enterprise-scale impact. The company's use of the business value framework ensured that every data investment served a defined business outcome. Then, the Data Centricity Framework helped determine what was feasible given the organization's current maturity and readiness.

This approach delivered several advantages. It brought structure to previously fragmented research processes, provided leadership with clear visibility into operational performance, and identified areas where targeted investments, such as Vendor and Prospect MDM, would remove friction and create measurable value. Each step in the roadmap was designed to build toward the next, creating momentum without overextending resources.

The impact came from how the capabilities were built; they were deliberately sequenced, fully aligned with stakeholder priorities, and tightly connected to business goals. BestBioSolutions now had technical, operational, and organizational capabilities to enable its growth and scale.

Summary

Let's summarize everything we've discussed so far into a pragmatic, business-first approach to creating a data strategy and roadmap that delivers on business priorities.

Step 1: Align with the Vision

Every business strategy (and data strategy is a business strategy first and foremost) must start with a clear understanding of the company's strategic vision: its long-term ambition and definition of success.

This is the step often skipped when data teams embark on creating a data strategy; the company's vision seems too high-level and too disconnected from day-to-day operations. So why start at such a high level? Because it creates a common understanding of the "why" behind the data strategy; without it, data investments can be reactive, fragmented, and easy to de-prioritize during a budget cycle.

When firmly aligned to the vision, the data strategy becomes a lever for executing on big bets, whether that's entering new markets, leading with innovation, or effectively and responsibly scaling. This step ensures your data work stays grounded in what matters most to the organization.

Step 2: Discover Business Value Using the Business Value Framework

Once the vision is clear, the next step is to translate it into specific areas where data can make a tangible impact. This is where the Business Value of the Data Framework comes in. It breaks down growth into four levers:

- More customers
- More products
- Better margins
- Acceptable risk.

It then maps them to specific, high-impact use cases. This process connects the abstract value of "being data-driven" to concrete business outcomes, connects these outcomes to necessary data capabilities, and lays the foundation for use-case-driven prioritization.

Step 3: Align Priorities Across Multiple Business Strategies

Most organizations have multiple business strategies in motion—such as new customer acquisition, cross-selling, cost optimization, digital transformation, and more. These strategies often compete for the same resources. This step ensures alignment and focus by identifying which capabilities intersect multiple strategies and business lines. It also forces the organization to make choices: which priorities are urgent, which are foundational, and which can wait.

Step 4: Determine Data Centricity Level

This is a very common "current state assessment" step, with one major difference: it extends beyond the technology state assessment to encompass operational and cultural aspects as well. This step is focused on understanding how the company currently uses data to operate.

Are we using data as an afterthought, a reporting tool, or a core to our decision-making?

The level of data centricity informs both what "minimal" and "viable" mean in the context of this company, that is, what can and should be done to deliver value quickly in a way that paves the way for long-term impact.

Step 5: Build a Roadmap for Common Priorities, Anchored in Data Centricity

With value identified, priorities aligned, and centricity level understood, the final step is to build a roadmap. This is a capability roadmap, and based on our definition of capability, it must cover not only technology but also operational and cultural aspects and it must be tied to specific business outcomes. It must show which data capabilities (governance, data integration, MDM, data quality, etc.) need to be built, in what order, to support the use cases that matter most. The roadmap has to be calibrated to the organization's data-centricity level, leveraging targeted, strategic steps that bridge the gap between the current state and the future vision.

To conclude, a data strategy succeeds when it directly supports business strategy through deliberate and ongoing alignment. Data capabilities should target specific business needs, not serve as a generic infrastructure. This focused approach transforms data from a mere tool into a catalyst for growth and innovation.

PART THREE

Applying the Frameworks

So far in this book, we've centered our discussion on for-profit companies and concentrated on building value-driven business data strategies and roadmaps aimed at enabling the organic growth of established for-profit companies. How does our approach change if the company in question is a nonprofit organization? Or a start-up? Do data capabilities play a role in an M&A scenario—that is, in cases of nonorganic growth strategies?

Let's answer these questions one at a time.

CHAPTER SEVEN

Mission-Driven Data-Driven: Data Management Strategy and Roadmap for a Nonprofit Organization

Not all firms are about profit. There are many organizations, including government agencies, charities, and member-based professional associations, that use (or should use) data to achieve their mission. Do the frameworks and approaches discussed so far apply to the nonprofit world?

Perhaps not surprisingly, they do, though with some changes in focus and wording. The most important changes are in the first two steps of our approach: vision alignment and business value discovery. Let's take a more detailed look at how to adjust these two steps. In the nonprofit world as well as in government agencies, member associations, and educational institutions, vision is often formulated as an organizational mission. Here are some notable examples:

The American Red Cross: *Prevents and alleviates human suffering in the face of emergencies by mobilizing the power of volunteers and the generosity of donors.*

National Aeronautics and Space Administration (NASA): *We reach for new heights and reveal the unknown for the benefit of humankind*

American Medical Association (AMA): *To promote the art and science of medicine and the betterment of public health.*

World Wildlife Fund (WWF): *Our mission is to build a future in which people live in harmony with nature.*

Harvard University: *To educate the citizens and citizen-leaders for our society.*

The nonprofit mission statement necessitates changes to the business value of the data framework. While different types of nonprofit organizations may have slightly different variations of this framework, here is a generic version (see Figure 16).

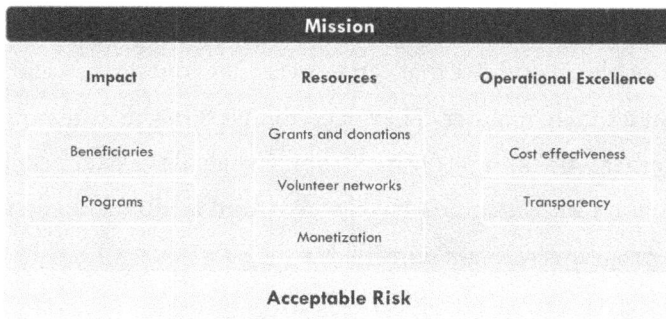

Figure 16: Framework for the business value of data–nonprofits.

To succeed in its mission, a nonprofit must define strategies for each of these pillars.

Impact centers on the organization's direct connection to the world it seeks to change. The effectiveness of a nonprofit's impact is closely linked to its capacity to understand both the population it serves and the mechanisms through which it delivers services. These two elements, beneficiaries and programs, constitute the core of the nonprofit value chain.

Similar to customers in the for-profit world, beneficiaries are the reason the organization exists. Nonprofits are established to serve a specific group or cause, whether it's vulnerable populations, students, animals, or ecosystems. That makes understanding the beneficiaries foundational:

- Who are they?
- What do they need?
- How do their needs evolve over time?

To achieve their mission, nonprofits must develop scalable and sustainable capabilities that can answer these questions accurately and in a timely manner. They need to invest in the infrastructure to gather, track, and learn from beneficiary data, such as demographics, outcomes, engagement, and feedback, so they can keep programs relevant and effective.

Similar to products in the for-profit world, programs are the primary mechanism through which nonprofit organizations pursue their missions. They function as the primary channels for delivering intended outcomes. The best nonprofits develop programs based on a clear theory of change, align them with their strategic priorities, and continually evaluate their performance. High-impact programs are typically characterized by their clarity of focus, adaptability, and reliance on data-driven insights. These programs evolve over time in response to both demonstrated successes and identifiable shortcomings.

What are the data capabilities that enable nonprofits to achieve an outsize impact?

Not surprisingly, it's the same set of data capabilities that drives value for the for-profit world: data governance to define ownership, roles, responsibilities; thorough and ethical data collection; master data management for beneficiaries and programs; data quality management of both beneficiary and program data; and, of course, AI, analytics, and reporting.

Resources are the nonprofit equivalent of revenue in a for-profit business. From a data management perspective, the major difference is that for nonprofits, the entities that are the most similar to customers (beneficiaries) don't pay for the services and programs they receive. This means nonprofits have an additional layer of complexity, since they have to manage two different sets of information:

- The first one relates to the beneficiaries who drive the impact.

- The second one relates to funding sources, which can include grants, donations, volunteer time, and even earned income.

Every nonprofit needs to know the answers to these questions:

- What are our current sources of funding?
- How stable and diversified are these sources?
- What would it take to scale them or replace them if one dried up?

Grants and donations function like recurring revenue. Some are restricted (more like earmarked project budgets), while others are unrestricted (akin to general operating capital). Both need to be cultivated and managed, including tracking performance, communicating outcomes, and ensuring funders understand the value of their investment.

Volunteer networks provide human capital, and just like employee engagement drives productivity in the corporate world, volunteer engagement drives capacity and reach for many nonprofits.

Managing volunteer information is yet another way in which nonprofits have a more complex world: while every company has to manage its workforce, understanding, managing, and effectively using the volunteer force is unique to the nonprofit world.

Monetization through earned income strategies, such as fee-for-service models, product sales, or licensing, can provide greater flexibility and sustainability. However, it also comes with its own risks, compliance, and ethical use requirements. For some nonprofits, it's a small supplement; for others, it's a growing line item that necessitates a business-model approach.

What are the additional data management capabilities that enable effective management of resources for nonprofits? Here, we encounter two additional data domains for master data management: donors, encompassing both individuals and organizations, and volunteers. These must be managed with the understanding that there could be a significant overlap between volunteers and individual donors, so both technical and organizational architecture (i.e., stewardship) must be carefully considered.

If monetization and data sharing play a role in the organization's operations, metadata management, as it relates to data rights, becomes key as well.

Operational excellence in a nonprofit setting serves the same purpose as in a business: to ensure that the organization can reliably, efficiently, and at scale deliver on its mission. The core disciplines are similar: cost management, transparency, and resource planning.

Three questions drive this domain:

- Are we using our resources efficiently?
- Are we operating in a way that builds trust?
- Are we planning far enough ahead to avoid crisis management?

In a for-profit business, cost-effectiveness or efficiency is usually measured by margins. The goal is to reduce costs and increase profits. Profit isn't a goal for nonprofits; instead, they optimize for the most effective use of their resources to achieve their mission. Counterintuitively, that may mean spending more on talent, technology, or data infrastructure, providing it enables better outcomes and scales the impact.

Transparency plays a role similar to compliance and investor relations in the for-profit world. Funders, regulators, and the public expect visibility into where the money goes and whether it's making a difference. Clear financial reporting, program accountability, and ethical operations foster trust, which in turn sustains funding and support over time. As in the for-profit world, the higher the level of data centricity of the organization, the more data and data capabilities can drive operational efficiency. While the data capabilities remain the same, establishing data quality at the source and implementing master data management at the point of sponsor, beneficiary, and volunteer onboarding are key.

Similar to the for-profit world, these three pillars rest on the foundation of **risk management.** Risk management in a nonprofit setting focuses on protecting the organization's ability to deliver on its mission consistently over time. Just like in the for-profit world, risk isn't something to avoid altogether. Some level of risk is necessary for innovation, growth, and responsiveness. As in the for-profit world, mismanaged risk can lead to dire consequences: loss of trust can result in loss of funding and, at the extreme end, may harm the very communities the organization is trying to serve.

There are three core areas of risk for nonprofits: reputational, operational, and privacy.

Reputational Risk

Because nonprofits are held to high ethical standards by funders, regulators, media, and the communities they serve, reputational damage can significantly impact the organization's ability to raise funds, build partnerships, and quickly erode support, regardless of program success.

Reputational risk shows up when:

- There is a mismatch between the stated mission and actual behavior.
- Stakeholder expectations are mismanaged or neglected.
- Ethical standards aren't upheld internally or by partners.

Managing this risk requires transparent communications anchored in data and metrics, consistent program delivery, and internal alignment on values. It also requires readiness to respond when something goes wrong. Organizations with a strong ethical foundation, a culture of transparency, and a clear accountability structure are more resilient in the face of public scrutiny.

Operational Risk

Operational risk refers to the possibility that internal systems, processes, or personnel fail in ways that disrupt service delivery or degrade performance. It's the nonprofit equivalent of a supply chain breakdown or IT system outage in the business world. For nonprofits, operational risks can include:

- Program interruptions due to staffing shortages or mismanagement.
- Inconsistent quality or delivery across locations or partners.
- Failure to comply with funder requirements or regulatory standards.

Nonprofits often operate with lean teams and limited redundancy, making them more sensitive to disruptions. For organizations delivering direct services, even minor operational failures can affect outcomes for beneficiaries.

Privacy and Data Risk

Nonprofits often handle sensitive data, including demographic, financial, behavioral, and even medical. Just like in the for-profit world, data privacy and cybersecurity are no longer back-office concerns.

But nonprofits face an added layer of complexity: many lack the in-house technical resources that corporations take for granted and yet are expected to uphold the same privacy standards. Key risks here include:

- Collecting more data than is needed (and storing it insecurely).
- Failing to obtain informed consent for how data is used.
- Inadequate controls around data access, sharing, or deletion.

Risk management relies on all the data management capabilities necessary to scale impact and resources with added emphasis on metrics, reporting, and analytics.

Depending on the mission and structure of a nonprofit organization, the relevance and weight of each value driver (impact, resources, and operational excellence) can vary. A government agency will prioritize different outcomes than a member-based association, and each will define success through a distinct lens. That variability is expected. However, what remains consistent is the need to anchor data strategy in mission execution.

To shift from frameworks to execution, I will now turn to a detailed case study: my work in building a mission-driven data roadmap for Best Friends Animal Society (BFAS), a leading national nonprofit organization focused on ending the killing of cats and dogs in American shelters.

Case Study: Creating a Mission-Driven Data Roadmap for Best Friends Animal Society

Step 1: Mission Alignment

Best Friends Animal Society's mission provided clear direction: "To bring about a time when there are no more homeless pets." The organization pursued this goal by helping to end the killing in America's animal shelters through the development of community programs and partnerships nationwide, working toward the rallying slogan of "Save Them All."

This mission statement highlighted three critical drivers for their business data strategy:

- **Primary focus**: Improving outcomes for companion animals
- **Core objective**: Lifesaving as the overriding priority

- **Operational approach**: Creating programs that enable animal shelters to save more lives

These drivers established the ultimate goal for their data capabilities: achieving better outcomes for pets, and thus created a clear prioritization framework. Additionally, tying data strategy directly to mission impact created natural buy-in and ownership from stakeholders across the organization.

Step 2: Business Value Discovery

During the engagement, BFAS was focused on an overarching initiative called No-Kill 2025, which was defined as a national commitment to end the killing of shelter pets by 2025. BFAS described no-kill as "a community commitment to saving every dog and cat in a shelter who can be saved." This concrete goal allowed us to identify specific areas where data capabilities could drive meaningful progress. Using a Business Value Framework, we mapped mission requirements to data needs across three dimensions: Impact, Resources, and Operational Excellence.

Let's begin with the **Impact** pillar.

While cats and dogs were the ultimate beneficiaries of Best Friends' work, the impact happened through animal care organizations, primarily shelters. To achieve No Kill 2025, the organization needed data capabilities that could answer three fundamental questions:

- **Which shelters need help?** Identifying at-risk shelters required access to reliable, timely data. One approach to obtaining that data was to manually reach out to each shelter, collect spreadsheets, and assemble ad hoc reports. While low-tech and shelter-friendly, this method was labor-intensive, inconsistent, and not scalable. Instead, automated and standardized data collection became essential. In addition to building API-enabled data intake pipelines, automation meant defining what data should be collected, standardizing it across shelters, and ensuring its completeness and accuracy. This introduced several core capabilities:

  o Shelter Master Data Management (MDM)
  o Metadata management for shared definitions
  o Data quality monitoring and issue management
  o Reporting and analytics to support decision-making.

- **What kind of help do these shelters need?** Help, in this context, meant programs. Determining which program suited a particular shelter required detailed knowledge about what programs existed, who they were designed for, and what results they produced. From a data standpoint, this introduced additional needs:

  o Program MDM: consistent definitions, unique identifiers, and governance for all programs o   Outcome tracking for programs across shelter types

      o   Reporting and analytics to match shelters to the right interventions.

- **What's the progress?** Once a shelter was engaged, BFAS had to monitor its advancement toward the No-Kill goal. Was the shelter enrolled in a relevant program? Was it seeing improvement? What obstacles remained? These questions required a unified reporting and analytics function built on top of clean, well-governed data from authoritative sources.

To summarize, to enable this impact-focused strategy, BFAS needed the following data capabilities:

- Shelter MDM
- Program MDM
- Metadata management for data definitions
- Data quality
- Reporting and analytics.

While not explicitly listed, data governance was threaded through each capability, establishing the roles, responsibilities, and processes that coordinate business, operational, and technical stakeholders.

Moving to the second pillar of the Business Value Framework—**Resources**—the focus shifted to sustaining the mission. For BFAS, this meant engaging donors and providing transparency into how their contributions are making an impact.

Like many nonprofits, Best Friends relied heavily on grant funding and individual donors passionate about specific programs. These funders were passionate about the cause and wanted assurance that their support was translating into real-world change. From a data strategy perspective, this created several requirements for transparent tracking of shelter progress, tied to donor-supported initiatives and robust reporting that demonstrated results.

It reinforced the need for strong Program MDM, as well as high-quality shelter data collection and ongoing reporting and analytics. It also added a requirement for Donor MDM.

Finally, the third pillar: Operational Excellence.

Here, the question shifted to cost-effectiveness and transparency. How did BFAS determine which interventions yielded the highest impact relative to cost? And how did it demonstrate responsible use of resources?

These questions required BFAS to deepen its understanding of programs—not just from an outcome perspective, but from a cost-efficiency perspective. This placed additional emphasis on Program MDM, which included cost dimensions and analytics that compared and projected intervention effectiveness.

Transparency also remained essential. Just as with the resource pillar, BFAS had to be able to produce accurate, timely, and relevant reports for both internal and external stakeholders. That meant continuing investment in enterprise reporting and analytics tied to high-quality, well-governed data.

Here is how the capability alignment map looked for the No-Kill 2025 goal:

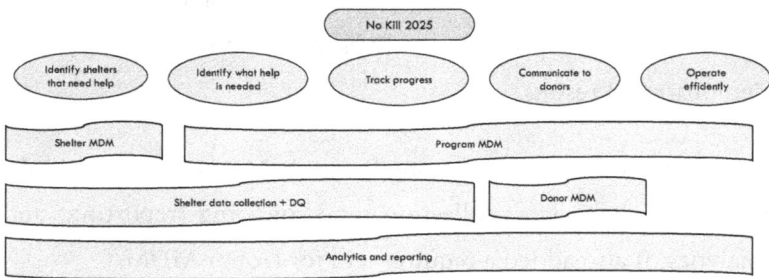

Figure 17: Capability alignment map for No-Kill 2025.

Step 3: Priorities Alignment

For BFAS, aligning priorities was relatively straightforward. The organization was tightly unified around a single goal—No-Kill 2025—and the entire business was organized to support it.

The prioritization matrix revealed a strong cross-functional consensus. Program MDM and analytics/reporting emerged as the top priorities across all departments. Shelter data definitions and quality followed closely behind, while Donor and Shelter MDM brought up the rear.

Steps 4 and 5: BFAS Data Centricity Level and Roadmap

The final steps involved evaluating BFAS's current data capabilities and determining the right starting point for implementation. How Data-Driven was its culture, and what capabilities did it already have in place?

What I found was that BFAS was very advanced, especially from a cultural perspective. Not only did it already have a system that uniquely identified donors and shelters and kept information about them up to date and connected to the operational and reporting functions, but it also had a robust Donor and Shelter MDM governance process. The business's participation in this governance process was unstinting; in fact, participation is not quite the right word to describe it—there was a strong business ownership and prioritization of these capabilities. There was also a strong analytics capability in place, again, not just from the technological perspective, but from a skillset, leadership, and visibility standpoint. Interestingly enough, the analytics, dashboards, and reports generated by this team were so widely used and so popular for such a long time that it created an additional requirement for the capability strategy: governance and metadata management for the analytical outputs.

This level of data centricity shaped a clear Phase 1 roadmap:

- **Workstream 1**: Program MDM. This was a great candidate for an MVP. On one hand, it had high alignment with the mission and the goal, high stakeholder engagement, and buy-in across multiple business drivers, including reputational risk mitigation. On the other hand, it had low technology requirements, which meant that it could be delivered and could start to bring value relatively quickly. Additionally, making a great argument for this being an MVP, was the fact that BFAS could chunk up program definition work: start with the biggest programs, test, and iterate quickly to scale the impact.

- **Workstream 2**: Data Quality on Shelter Data Intake: At the time of my work with BFAS, they were rolling out a new, automated, API-based shelter data intake platform. This created an opportunity to future-proof the quality of shelter data by incorporating shelter data definitions and data quality checks at the time of intake. Even better, the resources needed for workstreams 1 and 2 had a very small overlap, which meant they could proceed concurrently.

- **Workstream 3**: Reports and Dashboards Governance focused on rationalizing BFAS's extensive library of reports and dashboards, while introducing governance to ensure consistency, reliability, and clarity across all analytical outputs. Reports and dashboards rationalization was highly visible across the organization. Because of the wide reach and reliance on analytics at BFAS, even incremental improvements yielded significant benefits in terms of efficiency and trust in data. By embedding governance and aligning reporting outputs with mission priorities, this workstream provided a foundation for scaling data-driven decision-making across the organization.

This initiative complemented Workstreams 1 (Program MDM) and 2 (Data Quality at Shelter Data Intake) by ensuring that the high-quality data managed through those streams flowed into reports and dashboards that were accurate, trusted, and directly tied to BFAS's overarching goal of achieving No-Kill 2025.

Figure 18 shows a visual representation of the Phase 1 roadmap.

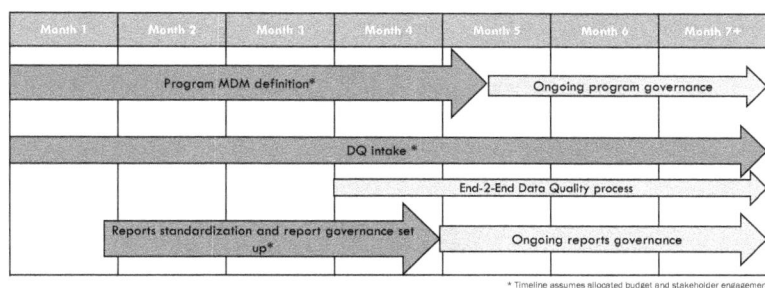

Figure 18: Data governance enablement Phase 1 work streams.

What about data governance policy and governance councils? These weren't ignored, but they weren't the starting point either. BFAS didn't need formal enforcement mechanisms up front because the engagement and ownership were already strong. Instead, policy and governance structures were intentionally deferred to Phase 2, once the teams had built and battle-tested new capabilities. By that point, governance would be easier to codify based on lived experience.

BFAS demonstrated a clear recognition of the importance of data. What was required, however, was a structured and mission-aligned framework to guide the prioritization, implementation, and scaling of data capabilities in support of their overarching objective—No-Kill 2025.

By grounding the data strategy in the organization's mission, linking it to measurable outcomes, and sequencing investments based on anticipated value, the roadmap we developed provided a coherent and actionable plan for advancing the organization's strategic commitment to Save Them All.

CHAPTER EIGHT

Data Management and Start-Ups

The Startup Advantage: Building Data-Driven Foundations from Day One

Most of this book focuses on approaches and frameworks for making data usable in companies burdened by operational, technological, and cultural legacy, organizations that grew up with data as an afterthought. But how do companies, even relatively new ones, reach that predicament? They defer thinking about data until it's almost too late, and they fail to establish a data-driven culture from the outset.

This oversight is understandable. Startups operate in a relentless race to ship products, acquire users, prove value, and secure the next funding round. In this rush, data often gets sidelined, getting treated as something to address *later*, once there's more money, more time, and more infrastructure to support it.

But that delay is a critical mistake.

> *Getting data right from day one represents one of the biggest advantages startups possess, yet it's also the one they leverage the least.*

Unlike established companies, startups aren't encumbered by years of technical debt, legacy systems, or siloed reporting hierarchies. They start with a clean slate. Yet most still choose to defer attention to their data until the mess becomes unavoidable.

What should startups do about data? Surprisingly, not much in terms of complexity or expense, but they need to think strategically from the beginning.

Let's look at a typical start-up journey and see what they should do about data and, more importantly, when.

The Startup Journey

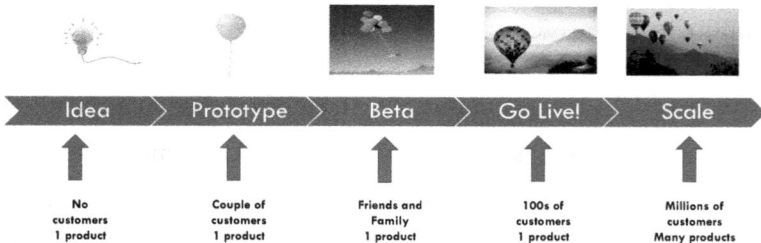

Idea	Prototype	Beta	Go Live!	Scale
No customers 1 product	Couple of customers 1 product	Friends and Family 1 product	100s of customers 1 product	Millions of customers Many products

Figure 19: From idea to scale–a startup journey.

Most early-stage startups follow a familiar path. The founders begin with a product idea—usually just one—and no customers. They assemble a team of believers, create an MVP or a prototype, and test it with close friends. If successful, they add features and progress to beta testing with a broader "friends and family" circle. Success there leads to the go-live moment, hopefully attracting hundreds of customers. Continued growth leads to the scaling phase, characterized by millions of customers and multiple products.

This scaling inflection point is precisely when useful, accessible data becomes critical, creating an enormous competitive advantage. Why?

To scale successfully, companies must keep their best customers satisfied, encouraging them to purchase more of their product and recommend it to others, creating a flywheel effect. This requires knowing:

- Who their most valuable customers are
- How to communicate effectively with them
- What keeps them satisfied and engaged.

Scaling also demands continuous product innovation while maintaining profitability, which means understanding:

- True product costs
- Profit margins by product and customer segment
- Customer profiles for each product offering.

In other words, scaling startups need all the information and capabilities we've discussed in the earlier chapters on sales acceleration and customer lifecycle value. Yet, if they first consider data capabilities only when they need to scale , they fall into the same trap as mature competitors: retrofitting systems to create data centricity. The startup advantage evaporates.

The Foundation Principle: Start Early, Build Smart

Here's the key insight: building a scalable data foundation at the beginning is easier and cheaper than at any later stage.

Implementing basic master data management with only a few customers, products, or vendors doesn't require complex technology or major reengineering. There are no live systems to refactor, no large teams to retrain, and, most importantly, no bad habits to unlearn. When companies put data at the center from the outset, the cultural foundation naturally develops. Product decisions, funding prioritization, and customer experience all develop from a data-driven perspective.

Four Foundational Moves for Data-Driven Startups

What does "getting it right" actually look like in practice? It begins with four strategic moves:

Move 1: Establish Data-Driven Culture from Day One

"Culture eats strategy for breakfast," as the saying goes. Put data front and center in every decision from the start, and never allow a "we'll fix it later" mindset to take hold regarding data. Treat data as a core component of building the business and bring in people who understand its value. Assign accountability and ownership for data the same way you assign P&L responsibility: there's no data-driven culture without business accountability.

Move 2: Build Customer Knowledge into Every Process and Product

Define and create a unique identifier for every customer from their first interaction with the company, starting as early as the prospect stage. This simple step eliminates future "Do we know who our customers are?" crises while sharpening the business growth strategy. Defining what constitutes a customer forces you to consider who they should be and what the ideal customer profile looks like.

Creating a common customer identifier is initially straightforward, with no expensive MDM platforms or complicated match-and-merge algorithms required. Focus on three essentials:

- **Add a unique identifier** at the first point of prospect or customer contact and carry it through every relationship, account, or transaction

- **Centralize onboarding** in one system, separate from product management or channel-specific systems. Don't create new onboarding mechanisms for each product, service, or channel. That is, don't create silos! This also saves time and money while accelerating time-to-market for new offerings.

- **Build real-time deduplication** into your onboarding system by requiring key information fields and resolving potential duplicates immediately while the person who knows the customer best is present.

Move 3: Apply the Same Principles to Product Management

Don't build product management systems assuming only one product exists. Create a product onboarding system even when it feels unnecessary, with just one product that everyone knows. It's perfectly acceptable to have a table with one row, as long as that product has a unique identifier.

When every customer purchase links a unique customer ID with a unique product ID, adding a second product immediately reveals which customers have both products, which have only one, and which remain prospects. This visibility becomes invaluable for cross-selling, customer segmentation, and product development decisions.

Move 4: Design Comprehensive Data Collection from the Start

Collect all customer data, not just what's required for basic product functionality. Tag customer interactions and product events with future analytics in mind. Think ahead to the questions you'll want to answer and design event structures to support analysis, not just logging. Include who did what, when, and in what context. The more consideration is given upfront, the easier it becomes to build effective reporting, analytics and, yes, AI, later.

Timing: The Optimal Window for Data Foundation

I recommend implementing these foundational moves during the prototype-to-beta transition. This timing strikes a balance between practicality and strategic necessity.

Acting earlier during initial prototyping often proves premature. The product remains too undefined, with a high probability of fundamental changes or complete code rewrites that would render data architecture investments meaningless.

Waiting until after beta, however, pushes the window too far. By then, customers are using the system, and if the product gains traction, the relentless pressure to ship features and respond to market demands intensifies. In this accelerated environment, data considerations inevitably fall by the wayside, relegated to the familiar "we'll fix it later" category.

The prototype-to-beta transition represents the sweet spot: the product concept has proven viable enough to warrant systematic investment, yet the customer base and technical complexity remain manageable. This window allows founders to establish data-driven foundations without the disruption that comes from retrofitting live systems or the risk of premature optimization.

Real-World Implementation: The Medici Case Study

I had the opportunity to implement these principles while advising Medici, a fintech startup. Following this blueprint, Medici strategically established three key pillars: scalability to accommodate various customer types, system design to efficiently handle multiple products, and comprehensive data collection across the entire customer journey. These pillars created the foundation for exponential growth and competitive advantage over rivals who overlooked these fundamentals.

The most remarkable aspect of implementing these foundational capabilities was the timeline. The entire process required just two hours of collaborative discussion among key stakeholders—me, the CEO, and the lead developer. In that meeting, we outlined customer journeys, identified essential data points, and drafted a data schema. After brief clarifications via Discord, these changes were integrated into the MVP without extending the go-live date or impacting development costs.

The Strategic Advantage of Early Action

This case illustrates the central paradox of startup data strategy: the solutions are neither complex nor expensive, but they require intentional thought and early action. Startups that defer data considerations until the scaling stage lose their primary advantage over established competitors: the ability to build data-centricity from the ground up, rather than retrofitting existing systems.

Startups that recognize this opportunity and act on it create sustainable competitive advantages that compound as they grow. In the race to scale, data-driven foundations often determine which startups successfully navigate the transition from promising concept to market leader.

CHAPTER NINE

Data Management in M&A

In M&A, data is often considered after the fact as something to be "integrated" later. But if we reframe the conversation using the Business Value of Data Framework, data becomes central to achieving the deal's objectives. Whether the strategy is to gain more customers, increase product penetration, improve margins, or scale without unacceptable risk, data capabilities can be either a multiplier or a barrier.

Let's walk through how data directly supports each growth lever, and what to evaluate during due diligence. See Figure 20.

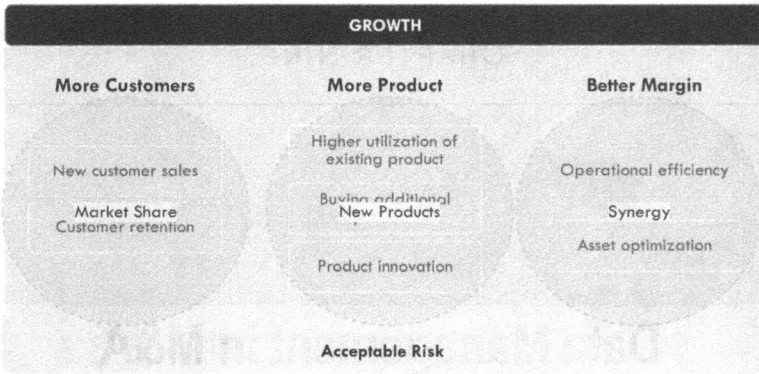

Figure 20: Framework for the business value of data – M&A.

More Customers: Can the Deal Actually Expand the Base?

A common reason for an acquisition or a merger is the expansion of an organization's customer base. By acquiring another company or merging with it, businesses aim to swiftly access new market segments, customer demographics, and geographic regions, far more quickly than organic growth would allow. As a simple example, let's consider a regional retail bank that aims to expand nationally. Rather than gradually opening new branches, which requires significant capital investment and time, the bank might acquire an already established institution in the desired regions. Through such an acquisition, the bank instantly gains access to a ready-made customer base, brand recognition, and local market knowledge.

Similarly, in the investment management industry, Morgan Stanley's acquisition of Eaton Vance in 2020 is a noteworthy example. This strategic acquisition enabled Morgan Stanley to significantly expand its asset management customer base, strengthen its product offerings, and enhance its presence in the retail investment sector. Eaton Vance's established client base and expertise in asset management facilitated immediate growth and diversification for Morgan Stanley.

How do data management capabilities play into the due diligence considerations in this case?

To capitalize on a new customer base and both retain their current level of business and cross-sell products, the acquirer needs to identify these customers, understand the overlap with their existing customer base, and develop effective sales strategies. Let's consider several possibilities for the target company in terms of its data maturity:

- **The target company is at the Data-Aware or Data-Informed stage:** To remind, this means that there is no common view of the customer across the enterprise. There may not even be a CRM system; the prospects and sales are likely managed in an ad-hoc manner. In the worst-case scenario, customer information resides on salespeople's personal phones and in their heads. If they decide to leave after the acquisition, all knowledge of the customers goes with them. If this is the case, the acquisition is unlikely to achieve its long-term goal of expanding the customer base. If no due diligence effort is focused on discovering the target's data capabilities, this could be a very unpleasant surprise after the deal is signed.

- **The target company is at the Data-Enabled stage**: That means that there is an enterprise view of customer and product data, and that there are well-developed organizational data capabilities, including extensive analytics and reporting practices. This is great news for the acquirer, as it means they can leverage these capabilities to achieve the acquisition's goals.

- **The target company is at a Data-Driven stage:** This is even better news for the acquirer, and the major reason to know about it before the deal is signed is not to lose it to a potential rival. Data-Driven companies come with broad data and analytics capabilities that not only make the realization of value from the acquisition much more certain but can also lift the capabilities of the acquirer and make their existing businesses much more profitable. That's worth paying a higher price for!

More Product: Can We Cross-Sell, Upsell, or Innovate?

Another common M&A goal is to expand products and uplift innovation.

Through strategic acquisitions, companies aim to quickly access new technologies, intellectual property, and innovation capabilities, significantly accelerating their product development timelines.

Consider the example of a tech giant aiming to enhance its artificial intelligence capabilities. Rather than investing considerable time and resources in internal R&D, the company may acquire a smaller, innovative firm, already pioneering advanced AI technologies.

As is the case with customer base expansion, the success of product-led mergers and acquisitions hinges significantly on the target company's level of data centricity. To effectively integrate new products, accelerate innovation, and ensure rapid market adoption post-acquisition, the acquirer must thoroughly understand the target's data capabilities and maturity. Let's examine several scenarios based on the target company's data maturity:

- **Target Company at the Data-Aware or Data-Informed stage:** If the target company operates at these stages, it is likely to struggle with fragmented data, lacking a centralized and reliable view of product information, usage, or customer feedback. Product data might reside in isolated spreadsheets, personal notes, or even informal discussions among product and sales teams. The absence of structured product analytics would make it nearly impossible to fully understand the existing product performance, user experience, or market potential. Consequently, and similarly to customer expansion-led acquisition, the acquirer would face significant barriers to integrating and leveraging the acquired products, thereby greatly diminishing the anticipated benefits of innovation or market expansion. Without rigorous data-focused due diligence, acquiring such a company might result in costly post-acquisition data reconstruction efforts and delayed or even unattainable integration of product lines.

- **Target Company at the Data-Enabled stage:** A target company at this maturity level typically maintains structured product data, employs consistent product management practices, and uses enterprise-wide tools to capture and analyze product performance metrics. This structured data environment empowers the acquiring company to quickly understand product performance, market response, and opportunities for enhancement or integration. It simplifies product rationalization and accelerates the integration process, enabling the acquirer to rapidly capitalize on the innovation potential and market opportunities presented by the new products. Acquisitions at this stage are generally lower risk, with clearer pathways to creating immediate synergies and market advantages.

- **Target Company at the Data-Driven stage:** A target company operating at the Data-Driven stage represents the most attractive prospect for product-led mergers and acquisitions. Such a company actively leverages advanced analytics, sophisticated customer insights, and robust product feedback loops to refine and innovate its products continuously. Acquiring it would not only provide immediate access to mature, well-documented, and highly optimized product offerings but also inject advanced data and analytics capabilities into the acquiring organization. The result would be twofold: rapid integration and enhancement of existing products, as well as a substantial uplift in the acquirer's overall capability for innovation. Indeed, the strategic value of a Data-Driven acquisition justifies a higher valuation premium, as it positions the acquirer to lead the market through accelerated product innovation and differentiation.

Synergy: Cost or Upside of Integration

Mergers and acquisitions can significantly impact operational effectiveness and margins both positively and negatively. On one hand, they can bring economies of scale and optimize resource utilization. On the other hand, different technology stacks can incur significant costs during post-merger integration and nullify the hoped-for synergies. And it's not just about technology. I've started this book by making a point that data capabilities go beyond the technology stack into organizational processes and company culture. Combining two organizations with different organizational and cultural views on data can create significant friction during the post-merger integration of business processes, operational roles, and a cultural approach to data centricity.

If the goal of the merger is to create a more efficient company, accessing data capabilities before the purchase can significantly impact the value of the deal.

Let's consider how the target company's level of data centricity impacts margins and operational efficiency post-merger:

- **The target company is at the Data-Aware or Data-Informed stage**: In this scenario, data is fragmented, inconsistent, and lacks centralized governance. Operational integration would be complicated and costly due to the extensive manual efforts required to reconcile and standardize data across different functions. These challenges would directly affect operational efficiency and could significantly delay the realization of cost synergies and margin improvements.

- **The target company is at the Data-Enabled stage**: When the acquired organization has already implemented structured data practices, consistent data governance, and reliable reporting frameworks, integration becomes substantially smoother. The acquiring company can rapidly capitalize on existing data frameworks, facilitating quicker operational integration and efficiency gains, which will positively impact margins soon after the merger.

- **The target company is at the Data-Driven stage**: A target at this maturity level provides the greatest immediate operational advantage. Data-Driven companies possess advanced analytics capabilities, real-time data-driven decision-making processes, and robust operational insights. These attributes would significantly expedite the integration process, directly contributing to substantial margin improvements through enhanced operational effectiveness and reduced integration costs. Additionally, acquiring such capabilities can elevate the acquiring company's own data maturity, multiplying long-term benefits.

In cases where the target company is in a Data-Enabled or Data-Driven stage, extreme care must be taken not to nullify the cultural and organizational advantages that come with this level of data centricity. Very often, after the merger is completed, the leadership and employees of the acquired company are on the chopping block. If the acquirer is at a lower level of data centricity, realizing resource synergies at the expense of the acquired company can significantly reduce the advantage of having bought them in the first place.

Acceptable Risk: Do Data Capabilities Matter to the Risk of the Acquisition?

No M&A strategy is complete without a view of risk. In this context, data can either de-risk or expose the deal. In addition to the now routinely considered information security posture and risk assessment of the target company, broader data due diligence is key for understanding other data-related risks.

As an example, let's look at how the target company manage its Personally Identifiable Information (PII) data. As in previous M&A discussions, data-centricity assessment of the target company helps to answer this question. PII data is all about metadata management and data governance—knowing what data is considered PII, where it resides, and who the business people are responsible for managing it.

If the target is in the Data-Aware or Data-Informed stage, it's highly unlikely that their metadata management discipline is robust. Even at the Data-Enabled stage, metadata management is often the most difficult capability to implement successfully and consistently.

As with other levers of M&A success, data due diligence is crucial to assessing the risk associated with the merger.

In conclusion, data management capabilities are as foundational to the success of mergers and acquisitions as they are to organic growth. Effective data management not only supports the achievement of core M&A objectives, such as expanding customer base, accelerating product innovation, and capturing operational synergies, but also significantly influences the risk profile of any acquisition. The degree to which a target company is data centric can dramatically enhance or hinder integration efforts, operational effectiveness, and the realization of anticipated synergies. Therefore, thorough due diligence focused on data capabilities is not merely beneficial but essential.

Companies that prioritize and rigorously assess data management practices throughout the M&A process are better positioned to unlock maximum value from their deals. Conversely, neglecting data considerations or assuming that they can be addressed post-integration often leads to unforeseen complications, cost overruns, and diminished returns.

Summary

Throughout this book, we have explored how data strategy, when grounded in business objectives, becomes a central enabler of growth. We began by identifying the four major levers of growth that are common across industries: acquiring more customers, selling more products, improving margins, and managing risk effectively. These elements are broadly relevant across sectors and serve as practical focal points for aligning data initiatives with business and organizational objectives.

We've also seen that data alone is not enough. For data to be effectively used in support of strategic goals, it must be accompanied by organizational structures, operational processes, and cultural norms that make it usable and useful. This is what I've referred to throughout the book as data capabilities. Whether it's ensuring consistent product management to support cross-sell, building client 360 to power retention strategies, or integrating multiple data sources to calculate customer lifetime value, the story is the same: business value comes not just from data but from the ability to use it.

I've illustrated this point across multiple case studies across multiple industries, including banks, an enterprise technology company, a biotech startup, a telecom company, and a mission-driven nonprofit. Each example demonstrated how data capabilities such as data governance, data quality management, and master data management contribute directly to achieving business outcomes. Although the specific contexts varied, the recurring need for foundational data practices was evident.

The case studies also served another purpose: they showed how to communicate the business value of data within organizations. Whether building executive support or aligning stakeholders, effective data leaders have to be able to translate technical investments into strategic outcomes. The case studies in this book are designed to serve as a guide for building your own value-driven strategy, helping to make the investment case, inform prioritization decisions, and establish common ground between business and data teams.

Finally, I return to the role of vision. A data strategy that is disconnected from a company's strategic vision will always struggle to remain relevant and to secure resources. But when aligned properly, data ceases to be a tech concern and becomes integrated into the core strategic fabric of the organization.

If you've read this far, you are already committed to making data work differently in your organization. I hope that this book has given you practical language, frameworks, and examples to do exactly that. Developing a coherent and effective data strategy is complex and context-dependent, but it remains a critical capability for organizations seeking to achieve long-term growth and resilience.

Let's get to work.

Index

www.ingramcontent.com/pod-product-compliance
Lightning Source LLC
Chambersburg PA
CBHW071556210326
41597CB00019B/3272